Anthropological Studies of Education

Series Editor
Amy Stambach
5230 W. H. Sewell Social Sci Bldg.
University of Wisconsin-Madison
Madison, WI, USA

This series examines the political, ideological, and power-laden dimensions of education from an anthropological perspective. Books in this series look at how society is defined in relation to education. It delves into the kinds of communities that are imagined through educational policies, curricula, institutions, and programming. Many books in the series use ethnography to capture diverse educational positions and experiences. The series uses concepts such as social practice, myth-making, political organization, and economic exchange to address substantive issues pertaining to education in the moment and over time.

Mehdi Galiere

Realities of Critical Pedagogy

A Microethnography of a Parisian Autonomous High School

Mehdi Galiere
Faculty of Humanities
Szeged University
Szeged, Hungary

ISSN 2946-3033 ISSN 2946-3041 (electronic)
Anthropological Studies of Education
ISBN 978-3-031-40265-4 ISBN 978-3-031-40266-1 (eBook)
https://doi.org/10.1007/978-3-031-40266-1

© The Editor(s) (if applicable) and The Author(s), under exclusive licence to Springer Nature Switzerland AG 2024

This work is subject to copyright. All rights are solely and exclusively licensed by the Publisher, whether the whole or part of the material is concerned, specifically the rights of translation, reprinting, reuse of illustrations, recitation, broadcasting, reproduction on microfilms or in any other physical way, and transmission or information storage and retrieval, electronic adaptation, computer software, or by similar or dissimilar methodology now known or hereafter developed.

The use of general descriptive names, registered names, trademarks, service marks, etc. in this publication does not imply, even in the absence of a specific statement, that such names are exempt from the relevant protective laws and regulations and therefore free for general use.

The publisher, the authors, and the editors are safe to assume that the advice and information in this book are believed to be true and accurate at the date of publication. Neither the publisher nor the authors or the editors give a warranty, expressed or implied, with respect to the material contained herein or for any errors or omissions that may have been made. The publisher remains neutral with regard to jurisdictional claims in published maps and institutional affiliations.

Cover illustration: © Fotomaton / Alamy Stock Photo

This Palgrave Macmillan imprint is published by the registered company Springer Nature Switzerland AG.
The registered company address is: Gewerbestrasse 11, 6330 Cham, Switzerland

Paper in this product is recyclable.

Contents

1 Introduction 1
   References 8

2 Official and Alternative Pedagogic Discourses 11
   Official Discourses on Education 12
   The Alternative Pedagogical Discourse in LAP 24
   References 32

3 Everyday Educational Practices in Paris Self-Managed
   High School 35
   Resisting the 'Blanquer Law' 37
   Debating Drug Prevention 42
   'The Orientation Days': Introducing the School to Outsiders 45
   Recontextualizing the Critique of Neoliberal Austerity 50
   Trust in an EFL Class 54
   Landscapes of LAP 55
   Voices in a Freedom Factory, *a Promotional Publication by LAP* 57
   Summarizing the Power Dialectics 61
   References 62

4 'Radio LAP': Recontextualizing Social Issues in a
  Transdisciplinary Critical Pedagogic Event   63
  Situating the Student Protest in the Neoliberal Economy 64
  Gender and LGBTQI+ Issues   71
  Migrations, Nuclear Energy and Strikes   78
  References   85

5 Conclusion: Rethinking the Collective and the Individual
  in Education Through Self-Management: A Generalizable
  Endeavor?   87
  References   96

Index   97

CHAPTER 1

Introduction

Abstract Against the approach narrowing down critical thinking as a narrow 'skill', which can be measured in terms of a reified idea of 'efficiency', the Paris Self-Managed Highschool or LAP (Lycée Autogéré de Paris) argues that critical thinking can only take place on the basis of democratic practices. It follows that LAP is embedded in the broader history of democratic education and is influenced by the theories of Brazilian educator Paulo Freire, notably by his critique of top-down 'banking pedagogy'. For Freire, banking pedagogy is a decontextualized and authoritarian way of teaching in which students' heads are empty 'banks' needed to be filled with 'what is best for them' from above. Through allowing for the self-management of the institution, in its mission statement, LAP intends to position itself as an integral part of the praxis of democratic education. How this unfolds on a daily basis will be the concern of the book, in which I carry out a critical ethnography that can be considered a 'critical theory in action', in line with the logic of critical pedagogic discourse. It is a critical praxis itself in so far as its goal is to reveal unfair relations of power hidden beneath the surface of what seems to be 'given', to take into account and acknowledge the critical expressions of different communities of practice as valid critique and to enact or inspire acts toward social justice.

Keywords Critical thinking • Critical pedagogy • Hegemony • Critical discourse studies

© The Author(s), under exclusive license to Springer Nature Switzerland AG 2024
M. Galiere, *Realities of Critical Pedagogy*, Anthropological Studies of Education, https://doi.org/10.1007/978-3-031-40266-1_1

Teaching 'critical thinking' is nowadays a commonplace in the value statements of educational institutions, from primary education to higher education. The French Ministry of Education, for example, dedicates various webpages and textbooks to explain the meaning and the relevance of the concept (Bidar et al. 2019; Ministère de l'Éducation nationale, de l'Enseignement supérieur et de la Recherche 2016). According to the French Ministry of Education (2016), 'critical thinking', the opposite of 'dogmatic thinking', is a skill and its transmission is mostly the goal of two isolated subjects: 'Media education' (*Education aux medias et à l'information, EMI*) and 'Morality and civics' (*Enseignement moral et civique, EMC*). In the Paris Self-Managed High School (*Lycée Autogéré de Paris*, or LAP), critical thinking is argued to be an outcome of critical pedagogical practices, rather than of the teaching of two narrow subjects. In other words, in LAP, critical pedagogic practices are argued to be founded on a democratic functioning of the whole school, and to encompass the broad range of educational activities organized in the school's context and in its environment.

Democratic education makes use of critical pedagogy and rejects the idea that teaching is a technical tool to achieve the 'transmission' of specific skills and that there are inherently 'bad' and 'good' ways of teaching, independent of the actual social context (Gay 2000). In his first book, *Pedagogy of the Oppressed* (Freire 1968), Paulo Freire, the founding figure of the field, criticized this dominant pedagogic practice of modernity and calls it 'banking pedagogy' (ibid, p. 53). The 'banking' practice is characterized by a top-down organization of the educational system at every level, most visibly in the classroom in which the curriculum is expected to be transmitted from the state to passively positioned students through the (equally passive because obedient) educators as if the students' heads were empty 'banks' needed to be filled with 'what is best for them' from above. My major interest is to investigate how critical pedagogic practices can be produced in opposition to practices of 'banking' pedagogy, and this is why I have chosen to do a case study of democratic pedagogy in the *Lycée Autogéré de Paris (LAP)*, or Paris Self-managed High School, as they claim to be an institution committed to the liberation and the empowerment of their students. LAP was initially founded in 1982 as a pedagogic experiment by the ministry of education. Today it is fully self-managed by its different actors and can welcome 225 students. In LAP, students are supposed to learn how school-based democratic practices shape broader democratic practices through practices of self-management instead of practices fostering competition of all against all. LAP is self-positioned against the ideal of a 'careerist' life. They argue that critical thinking must reveal such ideal as ideological. It is enmeshed in the hegemonic values of individualistic entrepreneurship and consumerism that Bernard Legros and Delplanque (2009) pointed out. In the Paris Self-Managed High School (LAP), critical thinking is argued to be an outcome of critical pedagogical practices, rather than of the teaching of two narrow subjects. In other words, in LAP, critical pedagogic practices are argued to be founded on a democratic functioning of the whole school, and to encompass the broad range of educational activities organized in the school's context and in its environment.

The LAP school is inscribed in a broader global movement of political resistance to capitalist authoritarianism through the implementation of democratic practices: the democratization of society has to be dialectically related to the democratization of practices in its educational institutions and in the definition of legitimate knowledge. That is, the practice of self-management is political rather than technical. In this sense, it shares similarities with experiments such as the Citizen School in Porto Alegre, a manifestation of the redefinition of citizen participation by the Worker's Party's (Partido dos Trabalhadores or PT) 'Popular Administration' of the city in the late 1990s (Apple and Gandin 2003, p. 203). Self-managed urban school settings are not that frequent in France, and already existing anthropological-ethnographic work on French education is usually limited to traditional schooling. For instance, Deborah Reed-Danahay, in her work on education and identity in France in the 1980s, chose to investigate the educational practices of a rural school community and its historical embeddedness in its immediate countryside context (Reed-Danahay 1995). Although my work shares similarities with hers as both studies focus on more 'marginal' schooling institutions and on the dynamics of power and resistance from these marginal positions, our approaches differ because of the contrasting situatedness of the two schools in both the class and spatiotemporal relations in French society.

My research draws on critical approaches to language use, pedagogy, and ethnography as I wish to privilege the agenda of the students and of the school for the creation of liberating knowledge at the level of interaction, instead of a technocratic agenda that analyzes and evaluates performance it in terms of a reified idea of 'efficiency'. This research is situated at the intersection of critical pedagogy (Giroux 2001; Freire 1968) and New Literacy Studies (Street 1995), which owe a lot to the Brazilian educator Paulo Freire. What these have in common is a discoursal approach to their field of interest that allows reflection on the broader social dimensions of classroom practices. In order to analyze the dynamics of power relations in the classroom, I draw on Antonio Gramsci's theory of hegemony (Gramsci 1971), Basil Bernstein's theory of pedagogic discourse (Bernstein 2000, 2003), Seth Kreisberg's theory of 'power with' (Kreisberg 1992), and on the insights from methodological approaches theorized by critical discourse analysis (Fairclough 1992, 2001, 2003, 2010), critical ethnography (Krzyżanowski 2011; Hammersley 1992), and microethnographic discourse analysis (Bloome and Carter 2014; Bloome et al. 2004).

The particular discourse I explore is pedagogic discourse, whose specificity, according to Basil Bernstein, lies in evaluating what counts as the relevant, appropriate or natural uses of language in pedagogic practices of teaching and learning. According to Bernstein's definition, pedagogic discourse consists of two constitutive discourses: a primary regulative discourse, that is, a discourse defining the social order and a secondary instructional discourse, classifying and organizing the knowledge to learn (Bernstein 2003, p. 92). In other words, pedagogic discourse functions to qualify what is thinkable or unthinkable in the educative field at a particular historical moment.

The approach I have applied is called *micro*ethnography because it is to observe and explore pedagogical discourses from within the local level of schooling. One way of exploring the relationship between the micro and macro levels, according to Karin Tusting, is investigating how (macro) institutional (national or supranational) texts are "coordinated" in the local language practices of education they intend to govern, or at least constitute (Tusting 2013, p. 6). This specific type of microethnography is called 'document analysis' (Bowen 2009): it consists of drawing upon multiple sets of texts to produce detailed descriptions and interpretations of complex events, organizations or phenomena. Document analysis is constructive as a means of triangulation—that is, 'the combination of methodologies in the study of the same phenomenon' (ibid., p. 28). In line with this logic of microethnography, I decided to choose 'macro-level' texts to be analyzed in this study, that is, the state documents regulating educational practices in the Île de France region in France, and the particular school texts produced in LAP mediating between state governance and local practices of teaching and learning. According to Glenn A. Bowen (2009, p. 32), one of this methodology's limits is the potentially biased selectivity regarding the texts to be analyzed since any collection of documents will be partial and important texts will end up discarded. Despite this drawback, document analysis allows for the establishment of a balance between data selection and data collection, which, in turn, can allow for the partial backgrounding of the investigator's presence in the research process (ibid., p. 31).

Microethnography is of the same epistemology as CDA: it aims to explore the dialectical relationship between broader social-cultural contexts and particular local events and institutions through the analysis of texts mediating that relationship. It claims that interaction at the local level does influence change at the broader level and reversely. My choice of microethnographic analysis of pedagogical discourse has also been motivated by the fact that it has been developed to explore critical literacy practices in both educational and community contexts, as theorized by Brian Street (Street 1995). Inspired by CDA, these scholars have developed the concept of the literacy event as a discursive site in which literacy practices of education are enacted through socially regulated interaction rather than existing as a static abstract grid or model to be replicated (Bloome et al. 2004, p. 6). According to Bloome et al., microethnographic discourse analysis conceptualizes an event as an emerging series of actions and reactions rendered into a particular pattern that people accomplish with one another at the level of (face to face) interaction. Such language use oriented ethnographic approaches, to use Karin Tusting's (2013) idea, insist on "the importance of participant observation in contexts", demonstrate "explicit reflexivity around the role of the researcher" and give a "central place to generating understandings of the emic perspectives of the participants" (Tusting 2013, p. 2). Linguistic ethnographic methods inform the so-called new literacy studies seen as a context-dependent social practice rather than a set of decontextualized individual skills (ibid., p. 5). It implies that the relevant methodological approach to understanding better how texts and discourses are received and (re)created in literacy events of education should focus on "contextual-to-textual macro-micro mediation in the analytical process" (Krzyżanowski 2011, p. 232). To this aim, ethnographic accounts of local literacy practices should explore the different trajectories of "texts and associated practices" from various macro and micro levels (Tusting 2013, p. 6).

I carried out my fieldwork in LAP between March 2019 and January 2020. I negotiated access to the school via email with the group responsible for the relations of the school with the outside world, particularly with journalists or researchers who would like to gain access to the school. My request was then discussed in a general assembly and accepted by the community. LAP is one of the two 'democratic pedagogic experiments' founded in 1982 by the ministry of education in the country, at the time directed by the French Socialist Party, the other 'experiment' being the 'Experimental high school of Saint-Nazaire' (*Lycée Expérimental de Saint-Nazaire*). Out of all possible alternative approaches to schooling, the self-management approach is the one I found the most relevant to analyze as it teaches what I consider one of the basic dimensions of democracy: allowing individuals to make decisions in the functioning of a collective that is based on relations of solidarity and equality. The choice of LAP over the Experimental high school of Saint-Nazaire was because I was not familiar at all with the functioning of the Saint-Nazaire school and because access to the field in Saint-Nazaire would have been personally more troublesome for practical reasons. LAP is fully self-managed by its different actors and can welcome 225 students. I had agreed with LAP that I would not use the name of the participants of the events analyzed unless specifically told to mention them. If the names are present in the written texts, I preferred to use them for the sake of clarity. I had full access to the field and could move freely in the school, talk to whoever was available and willing to have a discussion, whether they were students or teachers. Taking photos on the school ground was also allowed.

According to the statistics published by the school (Lycée Autogéré de Paris 2014, p. 27), the school population shows some telling tendencies. It is generally more male than female, which, they say, can be explained by the gender-specific behavior of the parents: "the fear of a certain freedom for the student, stronger among the parents of a girl than of a boy" (ibid., p. 32). Furthermore, compared to their ratio in the general French population, there are, respectively, fewer students whose parents are industrial workers or agricultural workers, and more students whose family background is related to the professional sphere of "culture and communication" (ibid., p. 30). This can be explained by the school's geographical context as, in the Paris region, "the industrial worker population has been replaced by service sector workers" (ibid.). Finally, the familiarity of students with the cultural and artistic worlds led them to be attracted by the school's artistic disciplines. All in all, the student population of LAP is a relatively older, aged 15–20, predominantly young male students attracted to art-oriented curricula, from a middle-class background. The students are sometimes giving up the comfort of going to nearby schools, spending a lot of time commuting by public transport to get to LAP. This population has often experienced schooling elsewhere as a form of 'violence' and moving to LAP expects different relations with adults and their peers (ibid, p. 31).

The set of texts I used for my case study consists of (1) macro-level documents representing education at the level of the governing body of the region and at the level of the school institution and (2) micro-level texts of different genres from local practices. Set (1) is made up of the Academic Project 2017–2020 (French title: *Projet Académique 2017–2020*) (Académie de Paris 2018) which frames the main guidelines and regulations of education in the Paris region for the years 2017–2020; set (1) also incorporates the School Project, authored by the staff of the school to recontextualize the state educational policy in their local practice while emphasizing the specificities of the LAP functioning (*Projet d'Etablissement*) (Lycée Autogéré de Paris 2014) and a collective book, published by LAP and authored by the staff and the students of the school, entitled *Une Fabrique de Libertés* (Lycée Autogéré de Paris 2012). Set (2) encompasses my observation of practices in LAP events such as the 'general assemblies' (assemblées générales, or AG) involving various school actors; semi-structured interviews with teachers and students about their representations of pedagogical and democratic practices in LAP and the relations between the school and the broader institutions governing it; five Radio LAP events I could analyze including one in which I actively participated, and diverse relevant 'non-educational' textual elements found in the school buildings such as posters. I had access to the macro-level documents in Data Set (1) on the internet with regard to the academic project and the school project, on the website of the Paris region academy and the website of LAP, respectively. The book *Une Fabrique de Libertés* was analyzed in its paper version, which I bought a copy of in a bookshop.

I compare the values presented in LAP's mission statement and their actual practices, taking into account the limiting fact that because LAP is an institution of the French ministry of education, pedagogic practice in the school is also situated in the broader context of state pedagogical practices. Indeed, the school also prepares its students for the national high school leaving exam, or *baccalauréat*, for which more conventional 'banking' practices of grading and testing have to be implemented. In the chosen school, I carry out a critical ethnography that can be considered a "critical theory in action" (Madison 2005) as such in line with the logic of a critical pedagogic discourse itself. It is a critical praxis itself in so far as its goal is to reveal unfair relations of power hidden beneath the surface of what seems to be 'given', to take into account and acknowledge the critical expressions of different communities of practice as valid critique and to enact or inspire acts toward social justice.

The argument unfolds in the following way in the book: in Chap. 2, the discourses on education articulated in the texts produced by the French State and LAP are analyzed. Analyzing these two texts together will allow for an interpretation of how the school (micro-level) institution articulates its educational discourse with regard to the expectations mediated through the regional expectation of the macro-level of the state discourse. The data sets analyzed in Chap. 3 deal with the actual practices in the everyday life of LAP. The chapter presents the analysis of the data collected in my fieldwork, namely interviews, observations and that of *Une Fabrique de Libertés* (*A Freedom Factory*), the promotional book published by LAP. In Chap. 4, the analysis concentrates on my involvement in 'Radio LAP', a weekly transdisciplinary pedagogical activity organized in the school. I especially focus on these radio programs because of their relevance for understanding the processes of recontextualization of different discourses in a potentially critical media and pedagogical discourse. The students' participation in running the radio program is a pedagogical event that should allow them to make full use of their creativity and position them as collective agents in the course of the production and organization of the weekly programs. The ultimate questions I intend to answer in my analysis in the subsequent chapters are (1) whether pedagogical practices in LAP contribute to reproduce or subvert social inequalities, in other words, to what extent the logic of neoliberalism is resisted in the pedagogical interactions, and (2) what kind of identities emerge in pedagogical practices in LAP and are legitimized, stigmatized or encouraged, by whom and for what purposes, in other words, to see if and how much the pedagogical discourse challenges the dominant identities in the state official pedagogic discourse.

References

Académie de Paris. 2018. *Projet Académique 2017-2020 de l'Académie de Paris*. Paris: Académie de Paris.

Apple, Michael, and Luís Armando Gandin. 2003. Educating the state, democratizing knowledge: The citizen school project in Porto Alegre, Brazil. In *The state and the politics of knowledge*, ed. Michael Apple, 193–219. New York: Routledge.

Bernstein, Basil. 2000. *Pedagogy, symbolic control, and identity.* Revised ed. Lanham: Rowman & Littlefield Publishers, Inc.
———. 2003. *The structuring of pedagogic discourse: IV, (class, codes and control).* New York: Routledge.
Bidar, Abdennour, Denis Caroti, Rodrigue Coutouly, and Gérald Attali. 2019. *Esprit Critique: Outils et Méthodes Pour Le Second Degré.* Paris: Canopé.
Bloome, David, and Stephanie P. Carter. 2014. Microethnographic discourse analysis. In *New methods of literacy research,* ed. Peggy Albers, Teri Holbrook, and Amy Flint, 3–18. London: Routledge.
Bloome, David, Stephanie Power Carter, Beth Morton Christian, Sheila Otto, and Nora Shuart-Faris. 2004. *Discourse analysis and the study of classroom language and literacy events: A microethnographic perspective.* 1st ed. Mahwah: Routledge.
Bowen, Glenn. 2009. Document analysis as a qualitative research method. *Qualitative Research Journal* 9 (August): 27–40.
Fairclough, Norman, ed. 1992. *Critical language awareness.* Boston: Longman.
———, ed. 2001. *Language and power.* 2nd ed. New York: Routledge.
———, ed. 2003. *Analysing discourse: Textual analysis for social research.* London: Routledge.
———, ed. 2010. *Critical discourse analysis: The critical study of language.* 2nd ed. London: Routledge.
Freire, Paulo. 1968. *Pedagogy of the oppressed.* Trans. M.B. Ramos. 2nd ed. London: Penguin.
Gay, Geneva. 2000. *Culturally responsive teaching: Theory, research, and practice.* New York: Teachers College Press.
Giroux, Henry A. 2001. *Theory and resistance in education: Towards a pedagogy for the opposition.* 2nd ed. Westport: Praeger.
Gramsci, Antonio. 1971. In *Selections from the prison notebooks,* ed. Quintin Hoare and Geoffrey Nowell Smith, Reprint ed. New York: International Publishers Co.
Hammersley, M. 1992. *What's wrong with ethnography? Methodological explorations.* London: Routledge.
Kreisberg, Seth. 1992. *Transforming power: Domination, empowerment, and education.* New York: SUNY Press.
Krzyżanowski, Michał. 2011. Ethnography and critical discourse analysis: Towards a problem-oriented research dialogue. *Critical Discourse Studies* 8 (4): 231–238.
Legros, Bernard, and Jean-Noël Delplanque. 2009. *L'enseignement Face à l'urgence Écologique.* Brussels: Les Editions Aden.
Lycée Autogéré de Paris. 2012. *Une Fabrique de Libertés: Le Lycée Autogéré de Paris.* Paris: Editions REPAS.
———. 2014. Projet d'établissement 2014-2019. https://www.l-a-p.org/wp-content/uploads/2019/01/Projet-d%C3%A9tablissement-LAP-2014-2019.pdf. Accessed 30 Sept 2023.

Madison, D. Soyini. 2005. *Critical ethnography: Method, ethics, and performance.* SAGE Publications.
Ministère de l'Éducation nationale, de l'Enseignement supérieur et de la Recherche. 2016. À l'école de l'esprit Critique. https://cache.media.eduscol.education.fr/file/Actu_2016/31/3/a_l_ecole_de_l_esprit_critique_680313.pdf. Accessed 30 Sept 2023.
Reed-Danahay, Deborah. 1995. Education and identity in rural France: The politics of schooling. In *Cambridge studies in social and cultural anthropology.* Cambridge: Cambridge University Press.
Street, Brian V. 1995. *Social literacies: Critical approaches to literacy in development, ethnography and education.* New York: Longman.
Tusting, Karin. 2013. *Literacy studies as linguistic ethnography. Working papers in urban language and literacies.* London: Kings College.

CHAPTER 2

Official and Alternative Pedagogic Discourses

Abstract This chapter covers the analysis of the French official discourse on education as articulated in the so-called Academic Project 2017–2020, a 32-page document issued by the regional governing body on education called Académie de Paris. The analysis explores the main commonsense understanding of the role of education and its different actors in the official (French neoliberal) discourse. Further on, I analyze the local discourse in texts issued by the LAP school, namely their so-called 'pedagogic project', in French 'Projet d'Etablissement 2014–2019', which functions in fact as the local curriculum; a requirement to produce by the State. The analysis of these two texts will make possible the interpretation of how the school institution articulates its educational practices with regard to the expectations mediated in the Academic Project 2017–2020 on the macro-level of State institutions and outsiders in general. It will be demonstrated that the managerial approach to the 'efficiency' of education characteristic of a market-oriented pedagogical model is rejected by LAP. At the same time, some aspects are left unquestioned, such as the desirability of the reified notions of 'competencies' and 'projects'.

Keywords Official pedagogic discourse • Alternative pedagogic discourse • Self-management • Interdiscursivity • Evaluation

© The Author(s), under exclusive license to Springer Nature Switzerland AG 2024
M. Galiere, *Realities of Critical Pedagogy*, Anthropological Studies of Education, https://doi.org/10.1007/978-3-031-40266-1_2

Official Discourses on Education

In France, the Ministries of Education (Ministère de l'Education Nationale) and of Higher Education (Ministère de l'Enseigement Supérieur, de la Recherche et de l'Innovation) and their regional institutions, the Academies, govern the educational practices in secondary schools and universities. The responsibility of middle schools is delegated by the state to the *Départements* territorial units, while primary schools are the responsibility of municipal authorities. Therefore, the Academic Project 2017–2020 (Académie de Paris 2018) is the relevant official document of guidelines for my analysis, the regional curriculum published by the Paris Academy, the region where LAP belongs. The curriculum document frames the purposes and functioning of education in secondary schools at the level of the Paris Region, it has been introduced as a result of the 1989 law on education (Jospin law) which delegated the responsibility of "defining the particular modalities of application of the national curriculum" to regional authorities, and required schools to publish pedagogic projects in accordance to these guidelines (Le Cor 2012, p. 179). The Academic project belongs in the official recontextualizing field, which is "created and dominated by the state for the construction and surveillance of state pedagogic discourse". This field differs from the pedagogic recontextualizing field, "consisting of trainers, teachers, writers of textbooks, curricular guides, specialized media" etc. (Bernstein 2000, p. 115). Both fields are relatively independent of each other and struggle for the control of what counts as 'thinkable knowledge'; they may form a consensus or may oppose each other (ibid.). Bernstein draws a link between pedagogical discourse and material reality when he claims that principles of recontextualization to be drawn from are diverse and that the selection of a principle among many others "varies according to the dominant principles of a given society" (Bernstein 2003, p. 184).

The official recontextualizing field is informed by the dominant neoliberal, or late capitalist, relations of production at the broader social level. Neoliberalism, also called the "post-Fordist", or "flexible" (Harvey 1992, p. 141) regime of capitalist accumulation, rests on flexibility with respect to labor processes, labor markets, products, and patterns of consumption" (ibid., p. 147). Neoliberalism consists in a "historically specific economic and political reaction against Keynesianism and democratic socialism" while extending the scope of the fields and activities to be governed by 'economic' values (Brown 2015, p. 21). In the educational system, neoliberalism entails a specific form of pedagogy the aim of which is to configure subjectivities toward the development of one's human capital (Holborow 2015, p. 15). Because "competition, not exchange, structures the relation among capitals" (Brown 2015, p. 81), the educational system needs to teach subjects on how to better adapt to the generalized competition in the perspective of improving one's employability. One symptom of this transformation is the increased importance of professionalization in the curricula, which subordinates the acquisition of knowledge to the acquisition of a normalized behavior supposedly common to all professional situations. This normalized behavior can be summarized by the concept of *transversal skills* (Laval et al. 2011, p. 95). The development of these skills would facilitate the adaptation of the subjects to the increased flexibility they will experience in the economic system (ibid., p. 96). Thus, neoliberal norms of employability define the ideal obedient, flexible and adaptable subjectivities required by the capitalist firms.

In order to show what the principles of recontextualization of the (neoliberal) material reality are, the analysis of the dominant pedagogic discourse will focus on the articulation of modality and identification in the text. These two categories represent the "commitments which people make in their texts and talk which contribute to identification – commitments to truth, moral obligation, necessity, to values" (Halliday 2013, p. 163). In other words, modality and evaluation analysis allows an understanding of the social actors' commitments "with respect to what is necessary (modality) and with respect to what is desirable or undesirable, good or bad (evaluation)" (ibid., p. 164). Although in the latter case desirability entails a modal assessment that extends "beyond the core of modality" (ibid, p. 183), and while desirability overlaps with modality categories, it is considered by Halliday as an effect of "comment modal adjuncts", restricted to indicative clauses and expressing the "speakers' attitude either to the proposition as a whole or to the particular speech function" (ibid., p. 190). Evaluation includes various linguistic means that do the ideological work of "implicit or explicit ways in which authors commit themselves to values" (Fairclough 2003, p. 171): evaluative statements, deontic modality (i.e., the modality signifying various degrees of obligations), affective mental process verbs (e.g. 'I like'), and value assumptions. Evaluative statements including devices of labeling and predication (Bloome et al. 2004, p. 104), in which case an attribute, such as 'horrible', expresses the evaluation of the carrier of the given attribute as desirable or undesirable, such as indexing desirability explicitly in 'this is wonderful' or more implicitly, like in 'this is useful' (Fairclough 2003, p. 173). The ultimate aim of the analysis is to explore what identities end up encoded as desirable in its discourse.

The Academic Project is a 32-page long document hierarchically divided in three main units, each called *ambitions*, claiming to recontextualize "ministerial orientations" at the "local level" of the given region. The authors call this aim "learning city" (*notre ville apprenante*) (Académie de Paris 2018, p. 2). The notion 'learning city' indexes an "economistic" neoliberal approach to knowledge production. It is neoliberal in the sense that it is oriented toward improving "the competitiveness of urban contexts in the global knowledge economy" (Plumb et al. 2007, p. 37), imagined to happen through maximizing "the willingness and ability of individual citizens to connect up to the flows of knowledge in the global economy" (ibid., p. 45). The three "ambitions" focus on the modalities of the 'pedagogical success' in terms of 'inclusion', the 'administrative management' in terms of 'evaluation' and the 'opening up of schools' toward 'innovation'. Inclusion, evaluation and innovation are thus represented as the main goals of the secondary educational system with regard to its adaptation to the so-called global 'knowledge economy'.

The three 'ambitions' are subdivided into *axes* and further into more specific "objectives" (*objectifs*). The principle of organization is hierarchical, representing the "objectives" as subordinated to the "axes", themselves subordinated to the "ambitions" of the Paris Academy. The three major units of ambitions include a list of 115 guidelines for education altogether, with each item starting with a verb in its infinitive form to attract the attention of the reader to some activity. The genre of governance of the document and especially its structuring into 'ambitions' and 'objectives' are characteristic of managerial texts and PowerPoint slides (Frommer 2012). According to Chiapello and Fairclough, the building up of meaning through additive lists, like the 115 objectives (Chiapello and Fairclough 2010, p. 270) "is inimical to complexity, analysis, and argumentation". This 'listing' has the effect of rendering the government's decisions as self-evident facts that are beyond discussion only to be 'ticked' like on a check-list. The combination of the paratactic format of listing and their introduction by the infinitive verbal forms suggests that every element of the list is equivalent and equally desirable, in other words, that the text is a kind of 'to-do list' oriented toward what 'ought' to be the educational practice in the region supervised by the Paris Academy. To give an example from each of the three 'ambitions', read Quotes 1–3 below (all the translations are by the author and the original material is available upon request):

1. To build a fair and ambitious school for all
2. To adapt the organization and the operating modes in order to better support the actors and the personnel
3. To reinforce and to valorize the openness of the school

As an institution representing state power, the Academy of Paris has a prescriptive function which aims at inculcating 'proper' ways of being and interacting, which, according to the key metaphor in the current document, is anchored in the broader instrumental representation of the city of Paris as a 'learning city' embedded in the 'global knowledge economy'. The reference to the 'global' context implicates a network of 'learning cities' across national borders that indirectly blurs the institutional boundary of schools as the sites of learning.

The various evaluations from the documents encompass the following categories: what the desirable and appropriate ways of being and (inter) acting are for the Academy of Paris, the producer of the document, for the school (i.e. school administration, or management at the individual schools' level), and for the actual teachers, the faculty in schools, and finally, for the students—rendered in that hierarchy by the logic of the document. In the introduction of the document, the authors tend to conceal their identity: 'the Academy' is blurred behind the notion of 'our project', inviting the readers, that is, the school managements in the region as 'one of us'. This apparently collectively authored documents then gives way to a naturalized hierarchy between 'us', the authors and the 'employees', sidestepping the hierarchy between the Regional authority and the school managements. The actor in many sentences of the check list tends to be 'our project' over the faculty and staff, such as "our project calls upon all the educational staff to […] reinforce social inclusion by providing a solid basis to the future learnings […] underlining the equal dignity of all types of training" (Académie de Paris 2018, p. 2), representing the educators, ironically, as a homogenous group of executors 'delivering' diverse types of programs that, unlike the workers, are assumed to have a dignity.

As this sentence demonstrates, the authors of the document in the Academy represent education as a de-skilling technical activity to be implemented from above, in a corporate manner. This activity positions the educational workers as if on an equal footing with the various types of education provided by schools in France. The value of the program's dignity is to hide the lack of dignity of the educators regarding their involvement in the formation of the Project. Furthermore, the 'dignity' is also underscored only to promote the vocational approach, that is, the approach to education as a means to gain skills of immediate relevance on the labor market, as legitimate. The vocational and general curricula will reinforce 'inclusion' because it is considered as a solution to mass unemployment. The idea that vocational training facilitates 'inclusion' is based on the instrumental economic assumption that 'society' is, to a certain extent, reduced to the labor market. This assumption is reiterated further on, this time framing the idea of inclusion in the context of the favorable ideas of "modernization" and "progress" required by a "constantly changing world"—while, in fact reinforcing the ever more top-down instruction of the school management.

The 'project' represents education as in need of guidance from the regional Academy:

> The project seeks to modernize and include schools in a continually changing world, to encourage autonomy of the actors [of education] [...] and reaffirms the necessity to guide the progress of the staff, as well as reinforcing the quality of service provided to the users of education. (ibid., p. 3)

To convince the readers of the validity of their arguments, the ideologies of 'innovation' and 'progress' are drawn upon by the authors of the project document. They argue, in a tautological fashion, that "every innovative project needs to develop a new work method", a new work method which consists of "discovering innovative experiments" (ibid.). The repetition of items from the lexical field of innovation and novelty seems to suffice to assert the validity of the argument, to the detriment of specifying what is concretely 'new' or 'innovative' in their approach. A hint of what is 'new' can be inferred from one of their objectives, which is laid out on page 20: "to adapt the continuous training [of school administration] to the new needs and to promote new modalities of training" (ibid., p. 20). Yet, the "new needs" are not specified, nor is specified whose needs they are.

The fact that throughout the document, the particular objectives are framed by verbal forms of action, enacting an identity of active agents committed to transforming the world. The Paris Academy represents its role as the ultimate authority whose manager role involves: "to improve the [educational] system's performance through a digital-technological based modernization" (ibid., p. 15); "build a solid and efficient organization" (ibid., p. 17); "modernize communication tools" (ibid.); "develop working in networks and projects" (ibid.); "elaborate a medium-term plan of action" (ibid., p. 18); "building guides and tools" (ibid., p. 3); "develop a new work method" (ibid., p. 3); "encourage the elaboration of collective projects".

The Paris Academy, as articulated in/by the above quotes, integrates the role of 'creator' or 'project builder' in a specific managerial practice labelled New Public Management, a "shorthand name for the set of broadly similar administrative doctrines which dominated the bureaucratic reform agenda in many of the OECD group of countries from the late 1970s" (Hood 1991, p. 3), which collapses the ways to run public and private institution in a single approach. Laval et al. explain the particularities of this managerial practice in the French educational system. They argue that the New Public Management is a managerial practice put in place in the public sector that entails a transformation of social relations with a focus on weakening the autonomy and the power of public sector workers (Laval et al. 2011, p. 36). The New Public Management of the neoliberal political economy, argues Laval et al., entails a twofold transformation. First, it replaces the specific values of the public sector by a standardized managerial culture based on some "fetishized formulae" such as "cost/benefit ratios" and "uniformized techniques of control" (ibid.). In the case of the Project Document, it is the fetishization of 'innovation' and 'projects'. Second, the technology of New Public Management transforms power relations between the public institutions and their workers and users by increasing the power of "managers" and "directors" of the economically 'autonomous' public institutions (Laval et al. 2011, p. 36). As a result of the transformation, the school leaders are positioned as 'managers' and their subordinated employees, the faculty are more strictly separated: the 'manager' is now entitled to force the change of the "archaic customs" of the educators to "modernity" through submission to "individualizing techniques of evaluation" (ibid., p. 37). Desirable ways of interacting between the state authorities and the educational institutions are thus centered on the evaluation of schools by the Academy of Paris through the new 'evaluation system' of individual school workers. The following list of technical procedures of managerial 'individual appraisal' based on the new evaluation system represents an enactment of a particular disciplinary approach by the Academy over the schools:

1. "encourage good practices" (Académie de Paris 2018, p. 17);
2. "lead the staff in their appropriation of new procedures" (ibid.);
3. "facilitate the exchange of good practices" (ibid., p. 18);
4. "develop the visits of education officers to valorize successes" (ibid., p. 19);
5. "strengthen the training of managers in conducting change and confident management to better lead the staff" (ibid.);
6. "better lead headmasters on the basis of protocols";

Evaluation to be performed by the Academy of Paris is represented in the document as a desirable process based on top-down managerial protocols, so-called "good practices" designed allegedly to bring 'success', particularly 'economic success' for the 'learning city' as clearly stated in the objective of bringing 'surplus value': "evaluate and increase the value of innovation, develop digital practices and the surplus value (*plus value*) they can provide" (ibid., p. 26).

The relationship between the development of 'digital tools' defined as a desirable tool of education and the creation of 'surplus value' may not directly be linked; the production of 'surplus value' is rather implicated to be achieved through a cost reduction. It is another question then to ask: How is the digitization imagined to achieve the surplus value? I can see two possible answers to it: the commodification of 'innovative' digital skills acquired by students or sold as privatized patents will give a competitive advantage to the 'learning city' in the global 'knowledge economy'; and digitization will allow for the reduction of the necessity of the school workers' physical presence at school thus allowing a reduction of public spending. Indeed, reducing spending in the public sector and in education is one of the main values expected of the New Public Management approach achieved by new state funding policies. It has been one of the main principles of the French state's economic policies for the past three decades, and its importance has been increasing since the financial crisis in 2008 (Laval et al. 2011, p. 43).

If the Academy of Paris presents itself as a managerial authority whose responsibility is to build a 'new' educational system in accordance with the 'new' ways of the world, it defines the school institutions as places in which "excellence and democratization have to go hand in hand" (Académie de

Paris 2018, p. 3). The objectives of the school, according to the document, are diverse. The schools should "fight inequalities" (ibid., p. 9) and "avoid the deepening of inequalities" (ibid., p. 7) by "pursuing equity" and "leading to success". For the Academy of Paris, the opposite of inequality is 'equity' (*équité*) rather than 'equality' (*égalité*). 'Equity' is a term that signals an intention, in French public policy, "to find a balance between equality and inequality" instead of actually levelling out inequalities (Burgi-Golub 1996, p. 76). Equity entails a configuration of inequalities that are considered fair and elevated to a social norm (ibid., p. 75). The 'fair' configuration of inequalities, that is, the equity principle the Academy of Paris applies to schools, consists in allowing students, albeit unequally equipped for the demands of the school system, to 'succeed' in their 'insertion' in their future professional lives. Schools will "encourage turning to partnerships to finance grants" (Académie de Paris 2018, p. 9); "increase the standing of the vocational curricula through promoting job training" (ibid., p. 13); "support [students] changing their career (*changements d'orientation*)" (ibid.); "to rely on relevant partnerships (National Education Citizens Reserve (*RCEn*) and Civic Service) and enhance the status of the partnerships in the surroundings of the school" (ibid., p. 21); "set down projects helping to develop the synergy between the content of the curriculum and partnerships" (ibid., p. 28); "develop mobilities to improve possibilities of professional insertion" (ibid., p. 29) and "distribute the linguistic offer based on the possibilities of professional mobility" (ibid., p. 30). Thus, to achieve equity, schools will have to promote vocational training and define projects of 'professional insertions' while relying on 'partnerships' with their surrounding potential partners, public or private.

In addition to this clearly defined orientation toward the market, there is also a strong moral orientation, or to use Bernstein's categories, an appeal to retrospective/prospective centering of identities along with the appeal to de-centered market identities. Two examples of 'partnerships' promoted in the document are the ones with the RCEn and with the Civic Service. The RCEn (The National Education Citizens Reserve, *Réserve Citoyenne de l'Education Nationale*) is a mechanism created in 2015 by the Ministry of Education inspired by the military reserve, after the Charlie Hebdo attack for which responsibility was claimed by the 'Islamic State'. It intends to promote the ideas of "republican values" and "secularism" in schools (Le Monde.fr 2016). The Civic Service (*Service Civique*) is a mechanism based on a voluntary commitment to work for a particular state-certified company or NGO, to "serve the general interest" and "republican values" (Le Monde.fr 2019). The Civic Service has been criticized by sociologists and left-leaning journalists for being a constrained choice for many recently graduated students who cannot find a job and thus forming a pool of underpaid workers, increasing the lack of job security (Le Monde.fr 2013). More explicitly, the authors of the document demand from the schools that they "strengthen the collective feeling of justice, security, belonging and cohesion" (Académie de Paris 2018, p. 16)—but never explicitly saying against what social ills threatening. Instead, they are expected to turn their students' gaze toward the 'glorious past' and "explain the importance of historical commemorations (*travail de mémoire*) through school competitions" (ibid., p. 29); Ironically, it is the management technique of 'competition' that is meant to resonate with the ideal of 'innovation' of the 'learning city' while the actual knowledge is that of the last century's national history and cultural tradition through the technique of "develop[ing] partnerships as a tool to participate in historical commemorations and great unifying events" (ibid.). The other value of 'project'-based education is implicated in the promotion of "support[ing] working on commemorative places from the immediate surroundings of the students (memorial plaques, statues, monuments). The Academy of Paris instructs schools to develop a student identity of telling hybridity: one that is based on teaching and glorifying a carefully selected past that serves to reinforce, in the present and among the students, a 'feeling of belonging' to a 'republican' community of the 'learning city', making use of digital tools legitimized by a neoconservative nationalist ideology. The ideological aspect of the 'republican' term in educational settings resides in the underlying undertaking to develop a "culture of silence" and of "conformism" among students instead of critical thinking (Biberfeld and Chambat 2019, pp. 161–62). The other element of this nationalism is racism. The glorification of the past in fact entails the glorification of a colonial past in French history curricula, according to Laurance Bieberfeld and Gregory Chambat. What the official emphasis of "republican" values evoke is the association of the meaning 'dangerous' and 'de-secularized' with parts of the country's mainly Muslim population which thus need to be 'civilized' rather than 'educated'. Consequently, the 'dignity' of the kind of training they may need is never to surface on the horizon of 'guidance'. The logic of the academy is caught in a utilitarian economic logic of budgetary authority, as the legitimation of underpaid jobs, the Civic Service, 'partnerships' and of 'glorious' local 'monuments' as part of educational practice can be understood as a dimension of cost-reduction policies. Indeed, costs are either externalized (partnerships) or suppressed (studying a statue rather than, for example, increasing the school budget for trips to the cinema).

The appropriate ways of being and acting of teachers and the faculty are situated at the intersection of a sort of mediation between the Academy and the students. Explicit deontic modalization is used in some objectives concerning teachers: teachers "have to develop all forms of ambitions" (Académie de Paris 2018, p. 7); "are called to cooperate with partners" (ibid.); "It is a necessity […] that they are able to adapt to new challenges" (ibid., p. 19); "their training must include the necessary changes of their profession" (ibid.); "renewing pedagogical practices seems like a necessity" in "a world in which the relation to knowledge and learning changed drastically" (ibid., p. 23). The instruction articulated for teachers by the Academy is to change, to 'adapt' to the 'challenges' of the world in which knowledge and learning are changing anyway. The 'cooperation' with relevant 'partners' ("the local authorities, associations, professional and economical actors" (ibid., 7)) is imagined to help the teachers to adapt and at the same time, to "fight against inequalities" (ibid.). However, they are never positioned as actors cooperating with their students. They are to 'receive' from above as much as their educators are receiving in a similar top-down manner from the Academy's document—the ideal 'faculty' is imagined to accept their subordination at the expense of their 'student'. However, their activity of teaching is presented as an act of 'coaching': teachers should "allow students to acquire school codes" (ibid., p. 12); "advocate strategies to develop the expression of talents" (ibid.); "popularize technological professions with girls" (ibid.); "help students to strengthen their motivation to choose his future career actively" (ibid.); "increase [students'] ambitions at school" (ibid.) and "foster the feeling of belonging through explaining the principle of secularism" (ibid., p. 21). The teachers' role is formulated as a type of 'pedagogical manager' who will lead students toward professional success and toward a 'feeling' of belonging in a secular nation. At the same time, in terms of racist ideology, the conflation of 'belonging' with a patriotic act of 'defense' of secularism against 'threats' aims at the suppression of religious differences especially targeting the Islamic faith which is associated with post-colonial subjects (Delphy 2015). However, as long as teachers are explicitly called upon to "incite project-based cooperative practices among students" (ibid., p. 10); "favor the project approach in learning" (ibid., p. 23); "favor innovative experiments in project-based approaches through involving students in developing their own social skills" (ibid., p. 26), the representation of pedagogical practice in the document naturalizes the unconditioned orientation to 'whiteness' and promotes the colonization of pedagogical discourse by managerial discourse. The relevance of the managerial category of 'project-based' approaches in pedagogical practices while tending to reduce the role of the teacher to an adaptable 'manager' located in between the Academy and the students is indirectly desirable for the faculty as well, as long as the 'teachers-managers' can see themselves as 'innovators' saved from the threat of precarity of the political economy and that of the 'Islamic' non-civilized colonial subjects. The document, therefore, can work together on managerial discourse of 'knowledge economy', with a neoconservative French nationalist and racist discourse of Islamophobia serving the aim of rebuilding the educational system as the site for the formation of a national community instead of a venue dealing on projects of actual social relevance.

The expected ways of acting and being of students suffer from a telling lack of clarity in the text compared to the desirable ways of acting and being at the administration and teacher levels. This can be due to the genre of the text itself, emanating from state authority to instruct workers directly subordinated to it. Yet, students are "asked to develop new skills of collaboration, autonomy, creativity, communication, digital skills, learning to learn [...] to be able to adapt to a world in constant evolution" (Académie de Paris 2018, p. 25); should "participate to historical commemorations and competitions in order to honor the values (*sic*)". In the name of knowledge, students are expected to learn a specific set of skills without any difficulty that will apparently facilitate their adaptation to a world in a natural motion of change. The skills listed are said to be easily applicable to the professional sphere and the workplace. In terms of interdiscursivity, the very definition of knowledge as a set of skills of practical reason implicate them to recontextualize in the pedagogic discourse from the professional sphere of management, positioning students of this digital communication as 'technopreneurs'. The apparent contradiction between skills and autonomy reflects the ideological configuration of the project-based 'new capitalism', in which autonomy comes to mean, for the agent, an 'autonomous' realization of specific tasks attributed to them in given 'projects', on which, ironically, they do not have the 'autonomous' power of decision. The "values" implied are 'flexibility' and 'autonomy' framed within the celebration of digital culture in itself, they resonate with the 'republican' and secular values alluded to in the rest of the document. The discourse of the Academy forecloses dialogicity: its discourse is consensual, hegemonic and silences alternatives. The main hegemonic assumptions it naturalizes are the existence of a 'knowledge economy' in which the appropriate way of acting is through competition, it also naturalizes the French republic as made of 'non-Muslim', 'white' subjects to reinforce the representation of the 'good' students as a homogenous group free from contradictions. Students are expected to be competing for skills, for access to higher education and to identify as part of a national community free from religious divides. A community they will have to help maintain the rank of in a world whose "constant evolution" is a natural process. The Paris Academy enacts an interpersonal identity of an 'authorized' agent, capable to 'manage' teachers, whose agency is limited. The high degree of modalization expresses a strong commitment to truth from the Academy, and a strong commitment to what the desirable and necessary ways of acting and being are in the educational system of the Paris Region.

The appeal to other discourses than the 'project-oriented' managerial discourse in the text is because, as Eric and Catherine Mangez (Mangez and Mangez 2008, p. 193) argue, the managerial logic of the corporate world, the "project-oriented Cité" or the discourse of digital capitalism as defined by Jodi Dean (2005), cannot translate into the educational sphere in the desired seamless manner. Indeed, the notion of competence which is at the center of the evaluation processes of efficiency in the managerial discourse is associated with more diverse justificatory principles in the school system than it is in the corporate world: in the project document, the reference to 'republican values' and the 'struggle against inequalities' involve a justification according to different principles than the "project-oriented" discourse: justifying the existing educational system through the prism of suppressing inequalities to allow for the 'success of all' belongs to the Civic justificatory regime, in which the 'collective will' is given highest importance (Mangez and Mangez 2008, p. 193). A combination of discourses also intends to make the Academic project more consensual through appealing to the various ethical and political sympathies of the actors involved in the educational system. Indeed, the need to justify the educational system as a device aimed at reducing inequalities is a hegemonic attempt to resolve or overcome difference with, to find common ground with, and forestall the "social critique" that can emerge from the agency of the actors in the educational system. The critique of these actors may foreground a representation of education as a collective good rather than as an instrumental responsibility for the individual, which is acknowledged by the Paris Academy in its particular dialogization of the discourse of 'social inequalities'.

The Alternative Pedagogical Discourse in LAP

This section focuses on the curriculum document called Projet d'Etablissement (School Project), authored by the staff of the school (Lycée Autogéré de Paris 2014). Publishing a 'school project', that is the local curriculum, is a requirement for every school according to French law, and it is required to define "the modalities of the implementation of the national curriculum" and to specify the pedagogic activities that will allow students to "succeed" at school (Code de l'éducation - Article L401-1 n.d.). I will explore how the text indexes the school's position as a self-managed alternative institution of democratic organization and how its actors represent the educational process in the school. The analysis of interdiscursivity, through the category of dialogicity will explore the voices that are drawn upon by the local school actors and through the category of assumption will trace down the pedagogical neoliberal discourse. The analysis of evaluation may explore what identities the local actors are negotiating for themselves, the students, parents and government administrators when defining the institution and its pedagogical objectives.

The analysis is interdiscursive in the sense that it is to explore the multiplicity organizing any given discourse. Texts are heterogenous, "hybridized", pieced together out of multiple representations, genres and styles resulting in discourse sufficiently different from their constituent elements (Fairclough 2010, p. 290). In any public sphere, such as the educational system, interdiscursivity is inevitable but what is open to negotiation is the organization of that multiplicity: whether it can foster "real dialogue" where participant 'voices' are in a symmetrical relationship to power (rendered into a relationship with one another according to the logic of 'power with') through winning the consent of the students, to the opposite end, where it fosters a "monologue" (of the classroom teacher or the principal), or even silencing, for instance, of all participants of education by the State. According to Lilie Chouliaraki and Norman Fairclough, "real dialogue" involves a symmetry of participants in their capacity to be involved in discussion, freedom to articulate the perspectives of everyone involved without stigmatization and an "orientation to alliance and to developing a new shared voice on the issue in question", while leading to action (attempting at reproduction or at transformation) (Chouliaraki and Fairclough 1999, p. 64).

Assumptions, on the other hand, can be 'afforded' by discourses of 'common sense', i.e. discourses emanating from positions exercising the social power to "shape to some significant degree the nature and content of this 'common ground', which makes implicitness and assumptions an important issue with respect to ideology" (ibid., p. 55). Fairclough distinguishes between three types of assumptions: existential assumptions "about what exists", propositional assumptions "about what is or can be or will be the case" and value assumptions "about what is good or desirable" (ibid.). The hindering or mitigation of intertextuality takes place through the systemic use of assumption, shaping the dialogicity of a text in telling ways. Fairclough argues that the actual degree of dialogicity is the effect of power relations (Fairclough 2003, p. 41). Dialogicity, that is, the degree of polyvocality in a text then comes about in the course of the negotiation of a text's orientation to difference in interaction. He differentiates between the following five scenarios concerning dialogicity, while insisting that they can get combined in any actual event, according to the possible configurations of power relations shaping the agency of subjects and the configuration of social structures:

(a) an openness to, an acceptance of, recognition of difference; an exploration of difference, as in 'dialogue' in the richest sense of the term; (b) an accentuation of difference, conflict, polemic, a struggle over meanings, norms, power; (c) an attempt to resolve or overcome difference; (d) a bracketing of difference, a focus on commonality, solidarity; (e) consensus, a normalization and acceptance of differences of power which brackets or suppresses differences of meaning and norms. (Fairclough 2003, pp. 42–43)

Hegemonic assumptions are the result of a consensus and an acceptance of difference of power as expressed by scenario (e), which consists of an absence of dialogicity, taking a particular representation as natural or 'given'. To explain the potential counter-hegemonic practices in the discourse of LAP, my analysis will mainly focus on scenario (b), that is, instances of accentuation of difference, conflict and polemic between discourses, on the opening of meanings of particular assumptions, and the representations, genres and styles it articulates. On the other hand, potential practices of 'power with' across different discourses, the articulation of discourses in such practices focusing on solidarity will be explained through the interdiscursive configuration represented by scenario (d).

The ultimate gain of the analysis of interdiscursivity is (1) an understanding of what dominant social groups seek in what ways to universalize or 'naturalize' what particular meanings as if 'common sense' while silencing others, reducing difference even to the point of silencing, in their own interests; and (2) how (much) these meanings are accepted, denied or challenged and if they are transformed through the textually mediated interaction of the participants. Critical literacy practices in schools self-identifying as alternative institutions, such as LAP in my case study, are a location in which the tensions between acceptance of, and resistance to, hegemonic meanings of 'good education' are possible to make visible through a CDA analysis.

The LAP school was founded in 1982 as a self-managed secondary school in which all staff members and students have an equal say in the decisions taken. It does not have a hierarchical division of labor as it has no headmaster, no cleaning personnel, nor kitchen personnel. Instead, al the tasks are the responsibility of the students and the teachers. The school community is made up of around 250 people at the time of my fieldwork. The common decisions are taken in small groups (GB, *groupes de base* or basic groups), who shape the agenda of the bigger AG (*assemblée générale* or general assembly) on a weekly basis. The evaluation policy of the school consists of an absence of grading, with an alternative system of UV (*unités de valeur* or value units) attributed to students according to their participation in the various tasks required for the proper functioning of the school (e.g. classes, groupes de base, general assembly). Because the school is funded by the State, it is required to follow the *baccalauréat*, or high school leaving exam, curriculum. It also has to publish a pedagogic project to detail their particular curriculum. The LAP school is independent when it comes to the selection of its students, who can come from anywhere in the Paris region or from the country in general.

The local curriculum, that is, the school project published in 2014 index and institution that sets itself up against what they see as an education of 'banking' articulated in the state and regional policy documents. 'Banking education' entails a hierarchy between the teacher, possessing the knowledge, and the students, a blank box to be taught, that is, in which to 'deposit' the knowledge (Freire 1968; Kreisberg 1992, p. 7). In other words, 'banking education' relies on the teacher/student contradiction, in which the teacher is placed in a dominant position vis-à-vis the subordinated student, and which reflects the oppressed/oppressor contradiction present in the broader society.

The authors of the School Project document argue that life in LAP is as "'real' as anywhere else" (Lycée Autogéré de Paris 2014, p. 3). In the text, the 'reality' of life in LAP "places into the background the search for efficiency and productivity which is often put into the spotlight in the professional world and in society in general" (ibid.). LAP dialogizes and accentuates a difference with the stereotypical assumed meaning of "real" in what is attributed to be the neoliberal state discourse of education, or at least to an ideological claim that an alternative approach education to the neoliberal instrumental one is 'not real'. Attention is drawn by LAP to the fact that the meaning of 'reality' is not limited to adapting to the imperatives of economic production as the dominant value of neoliberal education, rather, 'reality' can also mean questioning the dominant productivist ideology and foreground alternative values in the educational system.

Regarding the kind of social subject the education system is expected to produce, the concepts of citizenship and discipline are polemicized in the School Project document. The student as a citizen of the official policy documents in their understanding is seen as "the enthusiasts of strict definitions, heirs of a Jacobin doctrine on society" reduce the meaning of citizen to "citizen only in relation to the State", whose freedom only consists in "individual freedom" (p. 4). The metaphor "Jacobin" implies that in such representations, inherited from the French Revolution, the French society consists of a sum of individuals whose distinct individual freedoms and interests are embodied by a common and indivisible nation-state consisting of institutions of delegated and centralized power. Against this meaning, the authors propose a different definition of the citizen, one that is a politically empowered individual who forms part of a democratic collective. This is judged more appropriate in the context of their self-managed school. The authors argue that "it is possible to say that a student is a citizen" in the sense that "he or she can *participate in* the 'political' choices of the [local] institution. [...] This represents a step on the steep path leading to democracy" (p. 4, italics added). This is the core of the idea of self-managed education, which "aims at creating citizens who think critically" (Lycée Autogéré de Paris 2012, p. 12) and in which the "institutional dimension prevails over the pedagogic dimension in its narrow meaning" (ibid., p. 9). Therefore, educational practice in their understanding "is a political matter" that "horrifies the kind souls who sustain the myth of neutrality in education" (ibid.).

The school, as a public entity, is not only caught in the instrumental logic described above but at the same time suffers the managerial policies decided by the state. In the School Project document, the authors report the ministry's instructions they represent as "the system" (Lycée Autogéré de Paris 2014, p. 75): "now, we would have to continue our alternative project while applying the rules of the system (calculating the number of students per teacher, choosing optional subjects), a system admitting a will to fight its own failures!" Further, they argue that "it is a mystery for no one that a lot of 'young' people leave school 'with nothing' (according to their ready-made phrases)" (ibid.). The commonsense dimension of the ministry's discourse, qualified as a set of "ready-made phrases", is rendered by "it is a mystery for no one". The authors want to point out the contradiction between the aim of "the system", which is to "fight its own failures", that is, leaving "young people" with no positive outcome from schooling since they "leave school with nothing", and the austerity politics that impose a mathematical and managerial logic to presumably make education more 'efficient', thus allowing cost reductions. Managerial discourse is reported further on: "it is said that we could do the same thing (or even better things) with less: it means that useless activities have to be done away with". This utilitarian logic oriented toward cost reduction is then polemicized by the authors who propose a broader representation of education freed from its managerial constraints:

This logic silences elements that are not measurable in this manner, for example, to reconcile students with learning and with adults, to leave students time to think about their orientation, to allow students to find their way without being judged, to become self-confident and to access some kind of 'cultural diversity' (ibid.).

The position of LAP in the educational system is evaluated positively in the school project, as the school is argued to prefer "integrating" rather than the negatively connoted "excluding" students (Lycée Autogéré de Paris 2014, p. 8). To empower the students to "overcome" their fear of the scientific subjects like mathematics, physics, chemistry and biology, often seen as more difficult, is seen as a desirable objective albeit rarely achieved. The 'scientific' course is one of the three courses available in general secondary schools in France. It has the reputation of being the "perfect course" (*filière royale*) (ibid., p. 27) because receiving the scientific *baccalauréat* is supposed to open the way to most higher education institutions, and the texts do not polemicize this assumption. This evaluation positively appraises the instrumental reason considering secondary education as a gateway to higher education. This appraisal may be because the school project text is aimed at an institutional readership.

The membership of LAP in the Innovative State Schooling Institutions Federation (*FESPI*) is also valued in the School Project. FESPI is an association created in 2005 grouping together 17 state-funded educational institutions (as of 2024) sharing an 'innovative' or 'alternative' dimension. In the School Project, FESPI is argued to be a "place of exchange and reflection on our practices", "a way to emerge from institutional isolation", that allows "to pool our demands, to be supported by and to support educational teams if needed" (Lycée Autogéré de Paris 2014, p. 66). The authors assess that LAP and other FESPI members have the following values in common: they are fighting against school dropout, they have the willingness to "expand innovative practices", they can "assert their specificities" (ibid.). However, the authors realize that being committed to such values may clash with neoliberal austerity policies. They argue that LAP and other FESPI "innovative institutional" members "suffer" from the same disadvantages, that is, a lack of security concerning their status and the durability of the funding for their functioning. Aside from the FESPI, the LAP institution also participates in the "Self-management Fair" (Foire à l'Autogestion) organized by the Self-management Association (Association Autogestion), which aims at "promoting reflection and popular education on the set of themes around self-management" ('Qui sommes-nous?' n.d.). Participating in the Self-management Fair is positively valued as it "allows making progress on transversal questions raised during the practice of self-management" and allows "to have general discussions" on the theme (Lycée Autogéré de Paris 2014, p. 68). The "transversal questions" positively valued yet differ from the 'transversal skills' from the 'traditional' educational discourse. Examples of transversal questions are "general assemblies in self-managed cooperatives", "how to solve conflicts in a self-managed group", "internal power relations", "self-management and group sizes", "division and repartition of tasks", "self-management of struggles" or "popular education tools to discuss and decide collectively" (ibid.). The emphasis of these transversal questions is rather on empowering collectives through self-management than on transmitting individual skills as is generally the case in the dominant educational practices. In other words, authors of the School Project positively evaluate the fact of being part of networks whose purpose is collective democracy and empowerment instead of competition, the latter being the ultimate goal of networks in the managerial ideology.

The actual everyday practice of education is explained in the School Project document mostly through linguistic categories of evaluations conveying desirability and undesirability in educational practices, while interdiscursive hybridity is scarcely drawn upon. This is probably the case because the authors see their pedagogical practice other than that of the official one. Their approach can be best explained in terms of Bernstein's (1999) critique of traditional pedagogical discourse. The authors of the local curriculum document claim that their pedagogical practice embodies a weak classificatory principle when they say that "instead of an architectonic of disciplines and compartmentalized subjects, which knowledge structure can be pyramidal, we see the emergence of another model" (Lycée Autogéré de Paris 2012, p. 50). The pedagogic model they set forth consists of "an archipelago in which the competencies are islands communicating in networks" and replaces the "classical discursive rationality" by "a flow of knowledge coming from various places, and the "verticality of piled up knowledge" by "free horizontal circulation of knowledge" (ibid.). The way knowledge is selected, and to which ends, is not explained here. Horizontal organization is assumed to be a good thing in itself, although Bernstein warns that the selection of knowledge to be transmitted, albeit in an invisible pedagogic process, and the process of its recontextualization, all have a social basis and the acquirer is expected to learn a "gaze", a way of reading, evaluating and creating texts (Bernstein 1999, p. 163). In other words, horizontality can be progressive but also conservative when it is limited to instrumental market-oriented goals, such as the myth of participation through internet technology when fetishized as the ultimate solution for success in the job market, but in actual fact foreclosing any political consideration of that myth—as discussed by Jodi Dean (Dean 2005). Furthermore, the use of the term "competencies", abstracted from power relations, to describe a form of basic unit of knowledge in the LAP's document goes in the direction of Bernstein's 'generic' performance mode, which logic corresponds to the neoliberal requirements, as I have exposed above.

The School Project document details the specificities of the regulative pedagogical discourse in LAP in terms of the order it creates, the relations and identities produced as specified Bernstein (2000, p. 32). In LAP, the school practices are argued to "oblige" participants to put knowledge into practice by way of "working in teams and democratically conducting diverse meetings", such as the weekly decision-making 'basic group' and 'general assembly' meetings, in which the desirable ways of interacting are "to know how to listen, to know how to answer promptly while keeping a benevolent attitude and avoiding giving way to ones' frustrations" (Lycée

Autogéré de Paris 2014, p. 34). However, working in teams and conducting meetings are desirable practices in the 'banking pedagogy model' of the Regional document as well. What makes these practices different in LAP is the will to apply democratic principles in them. Trust is argued to be the ultimate intimation of all activities and all participants (teachers, staff and students) aiming "to get rid of the mistrust they often have towards adults from the world of education". In the local curriculum, 'trusting' the others serves to create a space where we can disagree, voice out differences and be open to the emergence of unforeseeable outcomes (Barát 2020). Trust in adults enables students to learn *savoir-exister*. The French expression translates into 'knowledge of good living manners' in English.

The School Project document also formulates the requirement for students and teachers to meet individually mid-year in February. These half-term meetings "allow" everyone to realize "what has been done, what has to be changed, what has to be improved or what has to be questioned (Lycée Autogéré de Paris 2014, p. 57). Students who "do not manage" to "blossom in the school" are told that "coming back at the beginning of the next academic year would not be good for them" (p. 57). Otherwise, students can take advantage of this "opportunity" to "redynamize his or her attendance at school", or to "establish a new life, educational or professional project" with the "help of his or her tutor and the Orientation Commission" (ibid.). Every student has a dedicated teacher, a 'tutor' who is supposed to be his or her referent during his or her schoolyears in LAP. The 'orientation commission' consists of two LAP teachers and of one guidance counselor who is not a permanent LAP member but is assigned by the State to visit the school if required by LAP. From this passage, we can conclude that, according to the authors of the document, tutoring is an "opportunity" for students and that 'establishing projects' with tutors and with a counselor is a good thing to do as it is hoped to help reorient the 'lost' student. The positive value of 'projects' seems to be assumed here as the ultimate means for regaining the student with no further discussion provided about the process and the project itself.

There educational practices in LAP are also regulated in the local curriculum with regard to teachers' and tutors' responsibilities in relation to students. Teachers are the "guarantors" of the livability of the "democratic aspect" of the school environment, which consist of "ethical, philosophical and practical" principles allowing for its institutionalization of a "democratic regime" of education (Lycée Autogéré de Paris 2014, p. 3). Three teachers are elected among their peers to form a "council" that will be in charge of relations with the Paris Academy, and this election is beyond reach for students (p. 10). Teachers "have to explain to new students" the specificities of the functioning of LAP during the first meetings at the beginning of the first year, for instance, the fact that the different domains of functioning of the school require the involvement of students to work properly, such as the cleaning, the restaurant or the basic groups. One aspect of it being positive evaluation in the form of 'Value Units' or *UV*. These units represent the basic division of pedagogic time, they are given based on the criterion of participation in school activities and they have to be distributed across a broad range of such activities to be valid. Every activity a student follows in the school year allows him or her to obtain a *UV*.

The polemic dialogicity in the LAP document reframes the purpose of education according to critical pedagogy: critical pedagogy is as real as 'banking' pedagogy, and it embeds the individual agent of education in a broader collective, going beyond his or her individual interests. The managerial approach to the 'efficiency' of education characteristic of a market-oriented pedagogical model such as the generic model is rejected by LAP. However, some aspects of the generic model are left unquestioned, such as the desirability of the reified notions of 'competencies' and 'projects', and whether this is an instance of reappropriation of 'generic' categories in a more 'radical' way is uncertain.

References

Académie de Paris. 2018. *Projet Académique 2017–2020 de l'Académie de Paris*. Paris: Académie de Paris.
Barát, Erzsébet. 2020. Populist discourse and desire for social justice. In *The Oxford handbook of language and sexuality*, ed. Kira Hall and Rusty Barrett. Oxford: Oxford University Press.
Bernstein, Basil. 1999. Vertical and horizontal discourse: An essay. *British Journal of Sociology of Education* 20 (2): 157–173.
———. 2000. Pedagogy, symbolic control, and identity. Revised ed. Lanham: Rowman & Littlefield Publishers, Inc.
———. 2003. *The structuring of pedagogic discourse: IV, (class, codes and control)*. New York: Routledge.
Biberfeld, Laurence, and Grégory Chambat. 2019. *Apprendre à désobéir: Petite histoire de l'école qui résiste*. 2nd ed. Paris: Editions Libertalia.

Bloome, David, Stephanie Power Carter, Beth Morton Christian, Sheila Otto, and Nora Shuart-Faris. 2004. *Discourse analysis and the study of classroom language and literacy events: A microethnographic perspective.* 1st ed. Mahwah: Routledge.
Brown, Wendy. 2015. *Undoing the demos: Neoliberalism's stealth revolution.* Cambridge: MIT Press.
Burgi-Golub, Noëlle. 1996. Égalité, équité. Les catégories idéologiques des politiques publiques. *Politix* 9 (34): 47–76.
Chiapello, Eve, and Norman Fairclough. 2010. Understanding the new management ideology: A transdisciplinary contribution from critical discourse analysis and new sociology of capitalism. In *Critical discourse analysis: The critical study of language,* ed. Norman Fairclough, 2nd ed., 255–280. London: Routledge.
Chouliaraki, Lilie, and Norman Fairclough. 1999. *Discourse in late modernity: Rethinking critical discourse analysis.* Edinburgh: Edinburgh University Press.
Code de l'éducation - Article L401-1. n.d. *Code de l'éducation.* Vol. L401-1.
Dean, Jodi. 2005. Communicative capitalism: Circulation and the foreclosure of politics. *Cultural Politics: An International Journal* 1 (March): 51–74.
Delphy, Christine. 2015. *Separate and dominate: Feminism and racism after the war on terror.* London: Verso.
Fairclough, Norman. 2003. *Analysing discourse: Textual analysis for social research.* London: Routledge.
———. 2010. *Critical discourse analysis: The critical study of language.* 2nd ed. London: Routledge.
Freire, Paulo. 1968. *Pedagogy of the oppressed.* Trans. M. B. Ramos. 2nd ed. London: Penguin.
Frommer, Franck. 2012. *How powerpoint makes you stupid: The faulty causality, sloppy logic, decontextualized data, and seductive showmanship that have taken over our thinking.* New York: The New Press.
Halliday, M.A.K. 2013. *Halliday's introduction to functional grammar.* 4th ed. New York: Routledge.
Harvey, David. 1992. *The condition of postmodernity: An enquiry into the origins of cultural change.* New York: Wiley.
Holborow, Marnie. 2015. *Language and neoliberalism.* 1st ed. London, New York: Routledge.
Hood, Christopher. 1991. A public management for all seasons? *Public Administration* 69 (1): 3–19.
Kreisberg, Seth. 1992. *Transforming power: Domination, empowerment, and education.* New York: SUNY Press.
Laval, Christian, Francis Vergne, Pierre Clément, and Guy Dreux. 2011. *La nouvelle école capitaliste.* Paris: La Découverte.
Le Cor, Camille. 2012. Le projet à travers des textes officiels de l'Éducation nationale. *Spécificités* 5 (1): 175–190.

Le Monde.fr. 2013. Le service civique, "choix contraint" de jeunes diplômés, 27 July 2013. https://www.lemonde.fr/education/article/2013/07/27/le-service-civique-choix-contraint-de-jeunes-diplomes_3451157_1473685.html
———. 2016. La « réserve citoyenne » remise au goût du jour?, 4 January 2016. https://www.lemonde.fr/education/article/2016/01/04/apres-charlie-la-reserve-citoyenne-a-l-epreuve-du-reel_4841222_1473685.html
———. 2019. « Le service civique est un moment-clé de l'orientation professionnelle », 23 May 2019. https://www.lemonde.fr/campus/article/2019/05/23/le-service-civique-est-un-moment-cle-de-l-orientation-professionnelle_5466181_4401467.html.
Lycée Autogéré de Paris. 2012. *Une Fabrique de Libertés: Le Lycée Autogéré de Paris*. Paris: Editions REPAS.
———. 2014. Projet d'établissement 2014–2019. https://www.l-a-p.org/wp-content/uploads/2019/01/Projet-d%C3%A9tablissement-LAP-2014-2019.pdf. Accessed 30 Sept 2023.
Mangez, Catherine, and Eric Mangez. 2008. Analyse Sociologique Des Discours Pédagogiques. Application Au Cas de La Politique Éducative En Belgique Francophone. In *Actualité de Basil Bernstein. Savoir, Pédagogie et Société*, ed. Daniel Frandji and Philippe Vitale, 189–206. Rennes: Presses Universitaires de Rennes.
Plumb, Donovan, Andrew Leverman, and Robert McGray. 2007. The learning city in a "planet of slums". *Studies in Continuing Education* 29 (1): 37–50.
'Qui sommes-nous?'. n.d. *Association Autogestion* (blog). https://autogestion.asso.fr/qui-sommes-nous/. Accessed 30 Sept 2023.

CHAPTER 3

Everyday Educational Practices in Paris Self-Managed High School

Abstract In this chapter, I introduce and analyze the various data sets collected in my fieldwork inside the school institution, such as my field notes from three 'general assemblies', classroom interaction in an English class, the posters and notes I noticed on the school grounds, a comic strip published by the school to represent an event of struggle between LAP and the State authorities, and half-hour long semi-structured interviews with different actors. The texts in relation to particular events analyzed in this section will be distributed into two main categories, broadly divided according to a macro/micro axis this time within LAP. I also analyze the promotional book published by LAP, *Une Fabrique de Libertés (A Freedom Factory)*, published by the school in 2012 to explain and promote its central values and functioning to the general public, the potential and actual parents considering the enrolment of their children in LAP and the prospective students. The discussion of these different sets of data foregrounded the issue of trust between students and teachers. The discussion determined that the passivity of students is taken for granted in most decision-making processes, which leads students to express themselves more freely in other spaces of the school, such as the common areas, or in specific pedagogical activities like classes.

Keywords Microethnography • Critical discourse analysis • Interdiscursivity • Evaluation • Identity

© The Author(s), under exclusive license to Springer Nature Switzerland AG 2024
M. Galiere, *Realities of Critical Pedagogy*, Anthropological Studies of Education, https://doi.org/10.1007/978-3-031-40266-1_3

The texts in relation to particular events analyzed in this section will be distributed into two main categories, broadly divided according to a macro/micro axis within LAP. The macro events will consist of practices concerning the broader functioning of the school: the internal practices of decision-making and of institutionalization in the event of general assemblies, and the outward-looking practices of participating in struggles in the more or less immediate environment of the school in political events such as demonstrations. The micro-practices will consist of the question of the struggles between the democratic school and the Paris Academy that will be tackled through an analysis of their recent conflict concerning the durability of current democratic practices in the context of austerity measures in the educational system. The data set that will be analyzed to such purpose is a transcription of an audio meeting between the Paris Academy clerks, a comic strip published on the school's blog and a press release published by LAP to inform the general public about the issue. Interviews and observations will allow me to also analyze an instance of drug-related internal conflict, classroom events, everyday interactions and details of the internal school environment.

General assemblies take place once a week in LAP, usually on Tuesday afternoons. They take place in a specific room designed for that purpose. They are the events in which most issues and orientations of the school are discussed by the whole community: this is the event where the self-managed aspect of the institution is the most salient. The general assembly is the main body of decision, and there is no other body that can administrate the school. Once a year, an 'information' or 'introductory' assembly is organized where potential future students are introduced to the functioning of the school. There is no relationship between the parents and the school unless the school community notices an immediate danger that would need contacting parents. The general assembly allows for "collective participation of school members in the process of decision-making" based on the rule of "one person equals one vote" (Lycée Autogéré de Paris 2012, p. 22). The smaller scale decision-making events involving a teacher and a smaller group of students are the *Groupes de base* (*GB* or 'basic groups'), and they are to submit issues on the agenda and discussed in the general assembly on a weekly basis. Teachers alone cannot bypass the 'basic group' structure to impose their own issues on the agenda. A 'basic group' event will also be discussed in this chapter to illustrate the dialectical aspect of direct democracy in the school, that is, how the general assembly and the 'groupes de base' are mutually influencing each other without being structured in a vertical, hierarchical manner. I will also focus on the issues of freedom and free attendance (*libre frequentation*) as experienced by the students themselves through an analysis of an introductory general assembly of the school to an outsider audience, interviews, and as explained by LAP in their collective promotional book *Une Fabrique de Libertés* (*A Freedom Factory*).

Resisting the 'Blanquer Law'

I have taken part in three general assemblies, and I made audio recordings that I later transcribed. A frequently arising matter in general assemblies during my fieldwork was and always is the participation of the LAP community in social struggles outside the school walls such as strikes and demonstrations organized by unions or other collectives, in order to defend the school's immediate interests or more remote ones. At an assembly during my stay on Tuesday 9 April 2019 at 2 pm, they discussed what strategy of the struggle the LAP should pursue against the new 'Blanquer Law' (from the name of the Minister of Education, Jean-Michel Blanquer) on the functioning of the *baccalauréat*—the high school-leaving exam. The law entails a reconfiguration of the available subjects of the exam and their modalities of evaluation: one of the main issues is that evaluation will be mainly based on continuous testing and grading rather than on a final test at the end of the last year of high school. In the assembly, almost all teachers and students of the school were present, even if only a few students spoke up.

One of the teachers, Pierre, presented a report that a call to a renewable strike had been launched, without specifying by whom exactly, against the new law. He added that this call had been "partially followed" by the LAP community and by educational workers in general. This partial presence of LAP raises the question of a stronger following, implying that calls from unions have to be followed by as many people as possible if they are to achieve their goals. He goes on to announce newer calls from the trade unions for the current week and their usual days, Tuesday and Thursday and the venues for gathering. Emphasizing the regular and planned aspect of organizing demonstrations on specific days could be a reminder for the LAP community present that they should already know and could plan their commitments routinely around these days to secure participation. He specifies that

> Today [Tuesday] there is a demonstration called by the 'AG Île de France' [the General Assembly of the SUD Education Union for the Paris Region, including all actors of education, faculty, staff and students] leaving from Nation square at 3pm towards République square; on Thursday there are many. I have heard about many meeting places, one in the morning in front of the education authority HQ (*rectorat*) and one in the afternoon yet to be defined as I haven't yet seen the exact place. (General assembly, 9 April 2019)

The recontextualization of the Union calls in the assembly meeting about the demonstration invites a debate about what should the appropriate reaction be. Two students, one sitting as a participant and the other acting as the moderator in the assembly, react by asking, "Shall we leave together for the demonstration?" The moderator takes up the question to ask all the participants whether the assembly should organize the school taking off to the demonstration. This is not a call to vote but opens the floor for arguments for and against. The teacher who introduced the union calls responds that the assembly should act as a collective body rather than as a sum of individuals, using the collective dimension to add authority to his suggestions: "We should try to manage this thing in a more collective way than asking individuals to decide whether they would go or not?" He then puts in perspective the difference between the two options by pointing out that the school has 230 people altogether, and that it's not with the participation of just 10 of them in a demonstration that it will change things. He goes on to suggest a strategy to secure a minimal presence at the week's demonstration and organize themselves, thinking up ways to increase LAP's presence in the meantime.

The emerging discussion involves three more teachers. Another teacher, Emma, replies that there is already a plan to go every Saturday to join the demonstration of the education-yellow vests. Here she refers to the demonstrations of the Yellow Vests which were organized every Saturday, and to the call to combine the struggle of the Yellow Vests with the struggles of the educational workers. Her argument implicates a disagreement that can be inferred from her argument voicing a financial concern. The participation in the potentially ongoing series of demonstrations against the new law may be beyond their financial means implicating that they overlap with their working hours: "It is expensive to demonstrate during our working hours", which means loss of salary for the participants. A third teacher, Joséphine, joins the debate pointing out the relevance demonstrations, arguing that she would not go to a small-scale demonstration: "I felt that the call to demonstrate does not catch on, the message doesn't pass". The usefulness of going to the demonstration is weighed up against the usefulness of being present at school. However, she argues that she is against only the one on the day of the assembly, but the one on Thursday would be different because the demonstration would be followed by a general meeting. Although she is convinced that they should "stop going to insignificant demonstrations", this time they should go and join forces "in front of the education offices and have a real group there". In other words, she also provides arguments and considers the location of the Thursday event, the education offices of the Paris Academy (*rectorat*) more of a public appeal. She also comes up with what LAP participants could do in the name of organizing, preparing themselves for the Thursday event—indirectly continuing her colleague's suggestion to organize a more prominent presence for Thursday: "We could discuss the texts we will write; we could also sing, we have this song we wrote, we could sing it". Although she does not specify the song but relies on her students' understanding of the reference to it, the presence of an already written song to use during demonstrations indexes the institutionalization of the demonstration routine in LAP practices. Thus, she discards demonstrations perceived to lack a clear call and message, like the one on Tuesday, the day of the assembly, and contrasts them with demonstrations with symbolic location (like the *rectorat*) and with more time and space for organizing.

The discussion is continued with another teacher, Michèle, lamenting on the fact that the protest against the new law involves only a few teachers and students, and they should think of strategies to make people feel involved. She suggests that the strategies could be elaborated in the coming weekly smaller committee meetings between teachers and students (*Groupes de Base*) which are the venues for grassroots organizing in LAP. Her contribution reinforces the trajectory evolving about investing their energies in the Thursday event. The discussion is concluded by two students from the assembly, relaying two more calls to demonstrate, both on Friday. One against police violence and the other organized by the Youth for Climate Paris and Désobéissance Ecolo Paris (*Ecological Disobedience Paris*).

These two calls are not discussed further in the assembly as the participants have indirectly agreed on one demonstration for the week. The topic is reoriented toward the 'Blanquer Law' itself by Pierre, the teacher who started the discussion in the first place about the two union's calls for the week. He complains about what he sees as the lack of commitment of the students to defend their school against that law and addresses them directly:

> I do not know if everyone realizes that if the reform is deployed [...], next year it will be too late to act, we will already be in the belly of the crocodile. (General Assembly, 9 April 2019)

Pierre further explains the various ways the reform is going to coerce the school into practices such as regular evaluation in grades and to limit its pedagogical liberties:

> We will have to evaluate you on many aspects, we will have to cram almost all the time, we will have less pedagogical freedom. (General Assembly, 9 April 2019)

The reform is represented as "a threat" for "us in LAP", a "crocodile" about to eat up the school with authoritarian methods, reducing the pedagogical freedom to adapt to the new law's criteria and reducing activities considerably to preparing "you", the students, for the *baccalauréat* exam through an increase in evaluation. This is a loss in comparison with the system before the change, only requiring evaluation during the final exam and not as a continuous practice. It is telling that the students remain silent in response to these accusations. This is a moment of hierarchical communication and not a moment of 'power with' as the teachers ('us') are argued to be more informed than the students ('you'), who do not understand what has to be understood according to the teachers.

This debate about demonstrations revealed that there is a significant difference in interests along the teacher/student divide about the desirable attitude in relation to social mobilizations. The union's calls about significant changes in the school-leaving exam and the changes they entail coming from above at the macro-level (national, regional) are recontextualized and are discussed in the local event, practically between teachers only. More interestingly, some of the teachers may have participated in some way in formulating the calls, as they are all union members I learned. The students seemed hardly concerned about the union's calls—the two students who moderated the assembly mostly structured the argument without providing additional elements. The two students from the audience, that is, not the two moderators, who participated in the debate shifted the attention toward different calls, more of concern to them than with the education reform of the State: police violence and ecopolitics.

However, as a consequence of the resolution of the assembly meeting on the 9 April 2019, a thematic 'Groupe de Base' discussion was suggested concerning the 'Blanquer law' for coming up with strategies of countering the reform and questions to be discussed by the broader collective in a subsequent assembly. Thus, the details of the 'Blanquer law' on transforming the *baccalauréat* were the topic of another discussion that took place in a general assembly on the 7 May 2019, to which I also went along. The fact that the 'Blanquer law' debate benefits from a continuation in the subsequent assemblies and not the demonstration concerning police violence and ecopolitics is telling in the sense that these latter interests seem to be backgrounded for the sake of the immediate struggle about the survival of the school. Students may seem more disconnected from the educational struggle as secondary school represents only three years of their life, whereas teachers are professionally committed to the survival of LAP and by extension to their material and ethical interests.

At the next assembly meeting, there were further moments telling of a conflictual understanding of 'trust'. In agreement with the previous week's meeting, the concern about the proposed new law is introduced in a question by a student, Xavier:

> since they are asking for a continuous assessment, will it be obligatory to give grades in a completely honest way and to put in place evaluation methods like in traditional schools? (General Assembly, 7 May 2019)

Béa, a teacher, is surprised by the use of the word "honest" in the question and observes that "LAP cannot see to favor its students [in the evaluation of their performance at the *baccalauréat*]. The student's wording assumes that the evaluation methods in 'traditional' schools are 'honest' which sets up the future (*sic*) evaluation in LAP in contrast, that is, implicating it as 'dishonest' but in favor of the students, as a possible option to limit the effects of the reform. If Béa is surprised by this assumption, Pierre recognizes the legitimacy of the question and argues that the "question of grading, we will have to answer … but we would prefer not to have it asked at all".

A third teacher, Benoit, gives voice to his stance indirectly through assuming the voice of the students and, in a heavily modalized way, that conveys uncertainty about his actual stance regarding grading:

Some students may think that since teachers will give grades, they may be a bit laxer than others, some students may feel like resting on this comfort, and I find it understandable. (General Assembly, 7 May 2019)

More interestingly, he reframes the assumption in the opening student question as an act of "defend[ing] the teacher's kindness, as if we are Santa Claus"? This is an ironic stance that entails not only distance between students and teachers but a critical stance from above by him. His argument, therefore, substantiates not only the logic of his argument but, indirectly, that of the legitimacy of his ironic stance: the initial pedagogical project of LAP and the different learning experience are about "doing things together". In this understanding, the act of grading is a problem that concerns the broader functioning of the school, and that teachers and students can resolve only if they act as a collective that would go against the very disciplinary nature of grading in traditional education. The paradox of ironic dismissal in the name of figuring out a collective way of grading is left unattended.

When a further date to discuss the reform in details outside of the general assembly in a special commission is discussed, the student acting as the moderator suggests an either/or option: "Who is going to join the discussions about the reform instead of going to the commissions on Thursday at 11 am?" Commissions are basic groups created for specific purposes, hence the creation of this temporary emergency commission concerning the struggle against the new law that will be held in parallel to the others. Seeing the hands raised by teachers only, Pierre reacts in a surprised yet weary manner "There are only teachers". A seemingly relieved student counters the teacher's words in an annoyed manner, counting the hands, that "There are actually three students ... there are ten students, it is fine. Eleven students". This conflictual situation tends to demonstrate that some students seem to disagree with their easy top-down labeling by some teachers as lacking interest for the struggle, and want to demonstrate this is not the case.

Debating Drug Prevention

Difficulties to take collective decisions between teachers and students involving the issue of trust was further exemplified during a debate concerning the creation of a new *groupe de base* focusing on the issue of drugs took place during the general assemblies of LAP on 7 May 2019. The concerned students, Mickael and Diane, introduced their proposition and intended to convince the audience of the desirability of such a drug-related *Groupe de Base*. One student involved emphasizes the necessity of such a *Groupe de Base* and its self-managed dimension. Mickael argues that they need a "really permanent thing" so that they could "manage this issue themselves" as "many of us have contacts with several organizations with whom we could work" and because "there is a need for this kind of group in the school". Another student confirms that "there is a real need for it because [...] we were asking who had been smoking at the park up the street and everyone said they did, there was not a single person who ...", before being interrupted by a teacher, Joséphine "this is not what I put into question, what I think I understand is that the group is about welcoming users of different products" which she contrasts with "the issue of prevention, limited to the reducing of risks". Mickael, the student, explains that if "there are so many people concerned it would be really good to have a permanent group with more time because if we limit ourselves to a workshop, it means it will not be something permanent". What is at stake here is the definition of the idea of prevention vis-à-vis drugs, especially marijuana, and the appropriate ways of dealing with the problem. For the students, prevention has to take into account the fact that the majority of students consume marihuana and that this situation requires more means to address the issue. For, Joséphine, the teacher who answered them, prevention means reducing risks at a general level and does not include, maybe for legal reasons, deliberately organizing meetings with students who are known to be drug consumers.

Another teacher, Pierre, recognizes the 'reality' of this discrepancy between the two representations of prevention: "I believe that we are pointing to two problems [...] is prevention limited to risk-reduction or is there something else? This is a real question that has been underlying in our school for a long time". The uneasiness expressed by this teacher is due to the way the external world may end up representing the school if the question of drug prevention is not answered, and what it involves for "the survival of the school": "if we are represented like a school in which there is a tolerance vis-à-vis drugs, we really are in trouble". To illustrate this, he recounts that "today at noon a student has been arrested by the police, they accuse him of smoking at the park, and unfortunately, I think they are right. I believe that unfortunately there are many students who smoke at school". Thus, he explicitly addresses the legal aspect that had been lightly touched upon by the previous teacher, leading him to define a difference between drug prevention and drug tolerance at school, out of fear of legal sanctions. Following this discussion, the creation of the new prevention-themed *Groupe de Base* is enacted by the assembly.

Conflicts also occur inside the school walls, and the analysis of the resolution of a particular conflict by the 'justice' commission, consisting of elected teachers and students, is going to be telling about how justice and disciplinary measures are negotiated in the practice of LAP, and how (much) relationship of trust are involved in the resolution of conflicts. In the assemblies, the issue of gaining trust between the teachers and the students is problematic as there is a tendency for teacher to approach this trust issue in a top-down manner. This particular conflict concerned transactions involving drugs in the school, and its story was told by a teacher, Béa, in an interview. She explains that a specific group of students decided to get elected to the 'justice' group by their peers, so that "teachers do not make use of their influence to solve conflicts". She qualifies this behavior as wanting to "gain some power, to achieve a 'subversive role' ", and that "some of them were not really aware of the rule that forbids possessing, selling or consuming drugs inside the school". When one of the students of the school, Paul, was caught selling cannabis in the school for the same time, Béa argues that she found it "interesting that the 'justice' group did not give any sanction" and that despite the school functioning based on dialogue, "students remained distrustful with adults" and that for students to admit that Paul is "known as a dealer at school" is not an appropriate behavior as it is "equivalent to be a 'snitch' ".

The second time Paul was caught, however, the 'justice' commission decided to meet to pass a harsher sanction. Béa claims that when teachers argue against some students' accounts banalizing the consumption of marihuana, asserting that it does not prevent them from participating in school activities, students accuse the teachers of speaking like "old people". However, when during this second 'justice' group meeting, Clément, a student member of the justice group, argued that there was indeed a "contradiction between daily drug consumption and being actively participating in the school practices", students listened to him in a different way as his approach was not perceived as a moralizing nor patronizing discourse by the students. The initial perception by some teachers of students participating in justice decisions as part of a play to acquire more scarce 'power' resource can thus evolve through practices of 'power with', in which students and teachers realize how, as a collective, they can think up more just solutions to conflicts. The dialogue between the teachers and the students evolved through the reduction of difference and the building of solidarity to achieve justice in this particular situation. Dealing drugs at school "endangers the community" according to the 'justice' group, who decided the exclusion of P, with a possibility of renegotiating the sentence at the end of the academic year. In her account, Béa qualified as 'subversion' the fact that students wanted to get involved in giving justice at school and show some 'tolerance' some drug-related behavior deemed unacceptable by her. Identifying the students' attitude as subversion disqualifies it and assumes the existence of an authority that has been subverted, an authority that comes to be associated with herself and the teachers' community. Eventually, when in her account, the students proved that they were able to manage the justice commission and resolve conflicts in a way that corresponded to what was deemed appropriate by the teachers, that is, when their behavior was not considered 'subversive' anymore, Béa considers that 'trust' has been restored.

'The Orientation Days': Introducing the School to Outsiders

I also want to include a 'general assembly' on 16 May 2019 in which three students, Ben, Kévin and Nina, and one teacher, Frederic, all from a basic group committee in charge of the relations between the school and the outside world (*Groupe de Base Accueil*) presented their school to an audience of potential future students and the persons who accompanied them. Their major objective was to explain how the actors of LAP represent and act the idea of 'freedom' in school practices. This time, exceptionally, the participants at the assembly were mostly non-school members and its objective was not concerned with organizing life at school and making decisions but in introducing the specificities of the school to an 'outsider' audience. The students were invited as they pre-registered on the school's website to be able to attend school at LAP from the following year.

The presentation was organized around the specificities of LAP's functioning and around the procedure to enroll. One of the main themes in the discussion was the kind of (inter)actions students are allowed to do in the specific context of LAP. In the students' presentation of the school, the absence of authoritarian practices of obligation that would limit freedom in the school is emphasized through the use of a low degree of deontic modality, that is called the "modal system of duty" by Derrin Pinto

(2004, p. 658). The notion of 'freedom of attendance' is used to illustrate the way 'freedom' is contrasted with a particular idea of 'obligation' manifest in more 'traditional' educational practices. Freedom of attendance is defined by the presenting teacher Frédéric as a practice that "really enables students to decide what they want to do at school". The three students elaborate that they can go to a class other than the one assigned on their timetable if they want to; they can change levels of education across three levels, *seconde*, *première* or *terminale*. In the French education system, secondary schools are 'chronologically' divided into three age groups: *seconde*, *première* and *terminale*. As a combined effect of these options, students may really schedule their own timetable. This freedom of choice is argued to enable students to make progress: "If someone is good at English, and he is in a class of *seconde*, he can very well go to attend a class of *première* or *terminale*". The presentation also points out the democratization effect of freedom of attendance on student-teacher relationships: "if you do not have any affinity with your teacher, which may happen, you can also switch classes" on the same level. Students want to reassure the audience that the particular educational practice in LAP they are explaining does not put into risk the ongoing activities organized in 'classes': "we are a secondary school, we have classes, don't worry". (General Assembly, 16 May 2019). The meaning of 'class' in LAP is not the same as the assumed meaning in 'banking education', consisting of an asymmetrical relation between teachers and students, the former possessing knowledge to transmit to the latter. Instead, the pedagogical discourse in the classes of LAP questions the traditional division rules in terms of time (age) and the authoritarian relationship between students and teacher in space: "we do not have a teacher writing on a blackboard with students sitting down in line, the teacher can sit anywhere, and the student can also sit anywhere".

The students from the *accueil* group also warn the audience of potential future students that 'freedom of attendance' is at the same time one of the main difficulties of the educational practice in LAP because it requires maturity and one can easily fall for the idea of freedom of attendance and not go to school on a regular basis. Also, the daily tasks that the collective has to take on such as cleaning, do the dishes, prepare lunch can be deterring because it may not be a habit for new students to be involved in this particular division of labor in a school. Yet, it is an obligation upon which depends the conviviality of the school atmosphere: "we are in a collective so we have to do it if we want to live in a more or less clean environment". In other words, the main difficulty is that schooling in LAP is not about passively learning subjects, like in the common practice in 'banking' education. Learning in LAP involves more diverse responsibilities.

The other specificity of their school the group present is the participation in the self-management of the institution. Self-management is the basic principle of the school, and according to Frédéric, it depends on the majority at school, that is, the students: "if people don't get involved, it doesn't work, out of two-hundred seventy people present at school there are two-hundred forty students, thus if students don't get involved, inevitably, the school doesn't function". He gives examples of self-management practices that would not function if students were not involved in them: "if there are no students in the *accueil group* like today, teachers can't do it by themselves, that's against the principle of self-management; same thing for the cleaning, for the kitchen, for plenty of other things". Being a student part of the school collective requires, according to Frédéric, "an important involvement [...], it requires involvement based on one's individual educational goal, if it is to obtain the *baccalauréat* then it demands an implication in [traditional] school work", and on top of that "it requires an involvement in all the other aspects of the life in LAP, in the projects, in the workshops, but also in the political management of the school, moments without which the school does not exist".

The students give details about the functioning of particular courses organized in the school, the "workshops" and the "projects". If workshops "can be switched during the year", and "can be created with or without a teacher", projects "are something that you have to keep along the year", which involves "defining a goal" which "we have to reach by the end of the year". If the term "project" seems to represent an instance of colonization of managerial discourse in the local practice of LAP to designate particular long-term courses, its appropriation by the students as something emanating from them rather than imposed from above mitigates its managerial dimension. Students also explain what the requirements to pass to the next grade amount to: "Value units are what allows us to pass to a higher grade, if we have twenty-four at the end of the year, we are obligatorily re-enrolled in the school". The only requirement about value units, according to Frédéric, is that "they have to be distributed in all school activities" for instance, "they can be obtained in classes, but also in workshops, projects and self-management", and that "if a student obtains fifty units from classes only, that is, if only classes are what interest this student", then it does not mean that the requirements are met. Indeed, a self-managed high school requires a different kind of involvement, which means that "if the student does not want to participate in the self-management, maybe he or she would be better off in a 'traditional' school in which students are better supervised when it comes to attending classes".

The obligation to graduate is also challenged and a possibility to not graduate is promoted: "we are a secondary school, we prepare for taking the *baccalauréat* exam, but if you do not want to take it, there is a class called *alternatibac*". However, the students presenting it do not wholly identify with this part of their school: "the timetable is totally different than ours", and while "they can do whatever they want", "we prepare them to do whatever they feel like doing without necessarily graduating" and one "can even participate in a first aid training". The 'us/them' opposition between the instrumental approach of those who wish to graduate and the approach of those who do not or cannot, although framed as a desirable possibility, is still represented in an instrumental, job market-oriented fashion. Indeed, "there are job-seeking workshops, training courses seeking, learning to fill out a CV, preparing for the *BAFA* (youth worker qualification) ... so it's pretty cool".

The discussion of the issue of graduation leads to a presentation of the potential ways the new reform of the *baccalauréat* may affect the functioning of the school from the following year. Frédéric introduces the school's opinion on the new law by referring to the reform in general and modalized terms as "a plan" that could have been accepted since it had a good potential; however, he ends up polemicizing with the government's text and explains that in spite of its "interesting" potential, it is eventually deeply caught up in the austerity politics of the State: "at the beginning, there may have been ideas in the reform plan that would have seemed interesting to us". He adds that the school staff realized that the reform was a negative thing as it contains "many things that go against our way of functioning" and as it is "above all aimed at the reduction of the school's workforce". The "interesting" ideas are not spelt out by Frédéric, who chooses to focus on the conflicting perspectives of the State's reform and that of the interests of the school. In Frédéric's representation, one of the main issues with the reform is that it goes against the schools' principle of not giving grades to students and of keeping an atmosphere free from competition, since the final grade for the *baccalauréat* exam and future affectations in higher education will rely in its majority on continuous assessing taking place during the whole academic year and on student rankings. According to Frédéric, there had been ways of resisting until then: "what we categorically reject, and it worked until now, is to rank students, we just put everyone as 'first', and it works". However, the obligation of continuous assessing will be less possible to avoid as it will be a core requirement to the *baccalauréat*, repositioning teachers as examiners instead of "pedagogues".

The other problem the representation singles out with the reform is that it will oblige students to select 3 specializations out of 12, whereas in the current situation, there is no such choice. The school will "have to make choices" about which of the 12 specializations to offer to students according to the 'resources' available to the institution. Frédéric closes on the possibility of contestation: although the school seems to have no choice, there is a hope that the reform can be adapted. The discussion of the *baccalauréat* reform this way takes the form of what Norman Fairclough would call a polemic dialogization of the State plan by the school. However, it is telling to see that it is only the teacher of the presenting group who can voice this 'hope'—drawing on some authority that is not available apparently for the students.

Finally, regarding the power dynamics, it is also important to reflect on the fact that the invited people could ask questions during the 90 minutes of the presentation but did not really have any, except at the end concerning the process of enrollment as such. The genre of this assembly was more of a one-sided lecture from the part of the presenters, the audience having the 'instrumental' expectation that by the end of it, they will be able to pre-enroll in the school.

The general assembly ends with the *accueil* group giving information to the audience on how to apply to the school. Frédéric highlights the fact that a test, a motivation letter and a CV are required in the application process so that the staff in LAP knows basic and relevant information about the students. The practices of selecting on the basis of a 'motivation' letter and a 'CV' are ironically managerial practices recontextualized in educational practices. The meaning of such practices in LAP, however, does not seem to entail a selection on the basis of labor market-oriented 'skills', rather, they seem to have an informative purpose for the teachers who will then make a final decision by themselves on which students are more likely to 'fit' in LAP.

Recontextualizing the Critique of Neoliberal Austerity

In May 2020, the Paris Self-managed High School got into a conflict with the Paris Academy concerning a plan of the Academy to decrease the resources available to the school. The cut into funding would entail a reduction in the number of taught hours in school. In turn, this would mean the withdrawal of a half teacher position in LAP. I analyze the press release by LAP related to this plan (Lycée Autogéré de Paris 2020d), a reappropriation of a comic strip in five parts, based on a comic book entitled *Le Retour à la Terre* (*Back to Earth*) by Ferri and Larcenet (2005) in which the text was rewritten by LAP members to illustrate the week-to-week unfolding of the conflict, and a transcription of the recording of an audio conference involving staff from LAP and their 'superiors' from the Paris Academy.

The audio meeting was between three teachers in charge of the relations with the Academy, and a civil servant from the Academy. It took place in May 2020 and was an audio appointment organized due to the impossibility to have a physical meeting because of the COVID-19 pandemic. In the audio meeting, the representation of the new development by the LAP teacher's is polemicized by the Paris Academy representative, that is, the LAP represents it as a reduction of the means available to the school, involving a reduction of teacher presence. Instead, the Paris Academy rejects the LAP's representation as something they are not allowed to say, and pushes forward its own representation of it as an 'evolution' resulting of a 'mechanical' process imposed by a legitimate authority, beyond any discussion: "you cannot speak of an elimination [of working hours], it is a mechanical evolution caused by the new law". Furthermore, the importance of the effects of this 'evolution' is downplayed, implying that LAP already benefits from a surplus of teaching hours compared to other schools. The LAP staff responds to the polemic that this kind of calculation is irrelevant to understand the self-managed specificity of their school and that "eleven hours represent half of the working hours of a teacher, that is half of his/her work and half of his/her presence". The Paris Academy argues in a moderately modalized way that the school is allowed to continue functioning as before on the condition that it adapts to the 'reality' of the resource reduction: "you can carry on working with twenty-five teachers, just by adapting your way of working".

The staff understands the condition as a request to partly work for free, as it would entail less resources but the same amount of work.

The Paris Academy argues, with a high deontic modality, that the school is obliged to come up with a clear plan ("clarification will be needed") on what specializations they will offer to students in the classes of *Première* and *Terminale*, according to the new law. Answering that, the LAP staff reports a quote attributed to the authoritative discourse the Ministry used to justify the law in order to point out that they conformed to the directives by wanting to offer a large number of specializations to students: "We have decided to offer a wide range of specializations to allow for 'students to choose their school career according to their preferences and ambitions' ". The Academy implies that such a wide offer is too costly and that the LAP school would be privileged vis-à-vis other high schools if it were to keep offering that many specializations to students. They also tell the school staff that the Academy is in a position of authority, allowing it to order the school adapt to the new requirements of the law: "Many secondary schools cannot afford such a wide offer of specializations, and I am an official vested with the minister's authority". The economic logic of the Academy is interpreted by the school teachers as a "bookkeeper" logic that does not take into account the actual needs of education nor society in general, that they do not specify here: "you are saying that the new *baccalauréat* allows for cost-cutting, you remain caught in a bookkeeper's logic while never thinking about the reality of the population's essential needs for education". At the end of the allowed 45 minutes of the meeting, the teachers close the conversation with "goodbye and see you soon, as we are not going to give up", a sentence interpreted as a threat by the Paris Academy, whose last sentence is "your threats do not have any effect on us".

This debate is based on a dialogization of the material consequences of an aspect of the new *baccalauréat* reform. The Paris Academy intends to resolve difference with the school so that they accept the requirements to adapt to the law, naturalizing the law as an 'evolution' in order to reach a consensus and close the dialogue. However, the meeting was called by the school to contest the law, to shift the dialogue toward a conflicting difference to have a say in the top-down approach of the Paris Academy in relation to the material enactment of the law which is evaluated by the school as a threat rather than as a simple 'evolution'. Although State authority is called upon by the Academy to impose a top-down consensus, no consensus is reached in this particular struggle between LAP and the Academy over the representation and the material consequences of the law.

This conversation and further meetings with the Academy were recounted in a five-parts comic strip. It was written by school members who participated in the audio negotiations with the Academy. The comic was addressed to the broader school community and to whoever was willing to support them in their struggle to keep the number of teaching hours unchanged for the following year. It was published on a blog specifically designed by LAP to keep a broader audience informed about this particular struggle against the Academy. The comic strip was published online in three separate blog articles, on 6, 8 and 10 May 2020 (Lycée Autogéré de Paris 2020a, 2020b, 2020c) (lutteslap.blogspot.com). I will only focus on the textual aspect of the comic strip. The focus on my analysis is the exploration of the interdiscursivity between the voice of the LAP as embodied by the teachers and the attributed voice of the Paris Academy. Compared to the audio meeting, the voices of LAP and the Academy are recontextualized as a fictive comic, in order to promote the struggle of the school and to render the voice of the Academy as a specifically antagonistic voice.

The first trip is an introduction that situates the current struggle in the history of the previous conflicts with the Academy. The character representing the school is named "Mme Self-management"; she defines the us/them polemical dialogicity between LAP and the Academy: "It is not the first time that they take away teaching hours from us, in 2011 they took away five full time working positions… five! That they gave us back eventually. But you will see, they are quite hard of hearing. Let's go!" The second and third strips relate the meeting with the Academy, in which Mme Self-management asks the two clerks at the Academy the following question, representing the decrease of teaching hours as an 'omission': "What is this thing with the forgotten hours?" The negotiation of the appropriate way to qualify these hours in the discourse of the Academy is rendered in the strip as "Well, one cannot say that it is an omission … I do not know whether you realize the difficult situation we are in". Immediately, Mme Self-management's voice removes the clerks' voice in the background, becomes the only voice present in the strip as if it were interpreting the Academy's discourse in a synchronized way, in order to dismiss it altogether as 'bamboozlement': "They do not seem to know what they are talking about […] they do not know anything about self-management that's for sure [...] I can see that clearly [...] they all seem to be agreeing on bamboozling us".

The two last strips, four and five, picture the reflections of Mme Self-management on the meeting that just happened. The representation of educational practices by the Academy is interpreted by the school as influenced by a certain managerial approach typical of the corporate field that entails cutting costs; also, the meaning of the term 'evolution' is polemicized and is argued to mean attributing more resources to education rather than taking them away: "they manage our schools like companies, they want to take away a half-teacher position, and they call it an evolution [...] They should support us and give us more resources, not hamper us! [...] An 'evolution'? It is a covered draining of resources instead [...]. The identification of Mme Self-management with a particular group of participants in the school, that is, with the teachers rather than with the students, is revealed in the last sentences of the strip, which finishes on a call to 'revolution' against the Academy's particular idea of 'evolution': "Moreover, they ask us to give up our extra hours, this means withholding part of our salaries to pay a colleague. Do they speak about 'evolution'? no way! [let's have] a revolution!" The identification of the main character of the comic strip with the teachers' community, yet as a spokesperson of the school's voice, can be interpreted as the result of the fact that it is the teachers (the adults) who are responsible for negotiating with their superiors from the Academy, that is, it is teachers who have access to that specific official field.

The choice of the comic strip genre illustrates a wish from its authors, the teachers, to speak to the students. Based on the analysis of the general assembly above where the reform was discussed and where some teachers were trying to convince the students to feel more concerned by the new law, the comic strip can be considered as an attempt to reach out to the students through other means. In the strip, the allegorization of self-management as a grumpy old woman translating the Academy's discourse on the reform to younger characters, and its identification to a wider group of 'colleagues', may illustrate a top-down patronizing approach from the self-proclaimed 'experimented' teachers, who, vested with an authority unavailable to students, do the work of 'negotiation', toward the students who have no choice but to rely on the teachers in such matters.

On 12 May 2020, following the audio meeting and the publication of the comic strip, a general assembly met online in order to issue a one-page press release to be sent to local media such as Le Parisien newspaper and to be published on LAP's blog (Lycée Autogéré de Paris 2020d). It situates the current struggle with the Academy as a result of the "principle of autonomy of school institution announced by the government in 2019" which entails "making difficult choices to share the resources in teaching hours among schools". The calculation of the available number of teaching hours per school, according to the authors of the release, "only corresponds to a 'bookkeeper's logic", that is, "the hour reductions are imposed in an authoritarian way based on the accounting spreadsheets [of the Academy] rather than based on the particular needs of the schools". That the Academy is attempting to make the LAP look like "a privileged school" in the eyes of the other schools to divide the struggles against the new reform is interpreted by the authors of the press release as "a refusal to understand the specific functioning of our high school", which illustrates a hypocrisy since even "two high-ranking officials in the Academy admitted that there is a need for full-time teachers in LAP".

Trust in an EFL Class

Relationships of trust between students and teachers were more salient during the English (as a Foreign Language, or EFL) classroom practices analyzed than at the broader level of the school, such as in the assemblies. I have chosen to analyze how classroom practices unfold in LAP and what kind of knowledge and interactions are legitimized in them. I went to observe English classes on two occasions. One of the most striking features of the interaction was the use of deontic modality (i.e., modality indicating necessity) by the teacher in order to sustain the pace of the classes, which can be qualified as a strong framing of pedagogical discourse. 'High' value deontic modality consisted of imperatives. It was mostly used by the teacher to delimit sequences in the classes in terms of space and time, such as "Now let's go to the computer room"; "this has to be done in three minutes"; "Let's discuss this orally, let's listen to each other"; "let's have a look at the different hypotheses". In other occurrences, deontic modality was used by the teacher but also by the students to keep a particular classroom atmosphere for teaching and learning, an atmosphere in which English is used instead of French whenever possible, in which students listen to each other and in which the pedagogical tasks given by the teacher are achieved: "Do this exercise"; "try to do the homework, it's [a requirement] not just a decoration"; "you had to work on this documentary, now we will put subtitles it will be fine"; "you just have to remember the grammatical rule"; "you will have to look on your phones"; "in English please" said by a student to another student who started to answer in French; or the teacher's requirement when ambient noise became too strong in the classroom "Calm down, it is really irritating now". The use of high deontic modality was more common in classes where students were tired, for instance, after lunchtime or on Friday afternoons. The teacher once argued that the students were "crazy on Friday afternoon after lunch; they are 'better' in the morning".

Lower degrees of deontic modality were also used by the teacher, expressing what people are 'supposed' or 'allowed' to do rather than 'required'. In this case, deontic modality seemed to have served to reassure the students by allowing for the possibility of not achieving all the 'expected' performances, thereby implying that the 'expected' performances consisted of, for instance, doing one's homework, taking notes, trying to understand or to express oneself in English: "Maybe we should agree that if there is homework you should try to do it […], it allows you to make some progress"; "it would be nice if, for next week, you could find a painting by Francis Bacon that you could explain to the class"; "you could try taking notes, anything, even words, so that you can get into it a bit more, it only lasts five minutes, it's not that long"; "I heard an interesting sentence, could you tell it to me in English? We should maybe write it down"; "Do you understand the sentence or do you want to translate it [to French]? Should we translate it?"

Landscapes of LAP

Outside the classrooms and general assemblies, the LAP school environment itself is decorated by a wide range of material, such as decorative posters, in common places such as the entrance hall or the cafeteria, where most students gather at one point or another of their school day. These materials illustrate the type of issues that their student authors would like to be more of concern in the school. In the entrance hall of the school, pinned on a board, an A4-format comic strip explains transgender identity through giving voice to a 'non-transgender character's' introducing himself in the following way: "Hi my name is Léo, and the sex assigned at my birth is the same as my gender, so we can say that I am a cis-man". To what the transgender character on the comic book replies: "I am a man too, but the sex assigned at my birth is different than my gender, so I am a trans man!" A particular discourse deemed hurtful and inappropriate (so-called 'war triggers') to interact with transgender people is recontextualized in a panel of the strip, named "War trigger: transphobia", and examples of inappropriate questions are given: "Are you trans, like in transsexual? Do you have a di**?", "Are you a real boy?", "Are you sure?", "how do you do to …?" Transphobic discourse is also recontextualized in a balloon, in which the character enumerates "a few things to avoid doing" when interacting with a transgender person: "Asking somebody's 'dead name' ", "questioning people's identity: a trans person does not necessarily have dysphoria nor does necessarily wants passing or transition, he/she is nevertheless legitimate" and "asking indiscreet questions about his/her body or sexuality". After listing these few examples of transphobic behavior, the character requests the reader to respect the identity of transgender people, in a specific 'youth' slang to convey solidarity: "so, use my pronoun(s) and my name!! 'Heart on you' ". This comic strip's intention is to avoid any kind of bullying or discrimination against transgender students who attend the school. It delegitimizes particular behaviors and interactional patterns by exposing their stigmatizing and hurtful dimension for people self-identifying as transgender.

In another busy space of the school, the cafeteria, two big size hand-drawn posters were displayed, one explaining the word *tafiole* (faggot) as "a combination between *tapette* (fag) and *folle* (queen), vulgar way to define a homosexual male", in order to make readers realize why it is part of homophobic hate speech, thus why its usage is inappropriate in the school and in society in general. A second poster instructs the reader to take the wasted food or would-be wasted food from supermarkets such as Auchan and Carrefour (the two biggest supermarket chains in France) whose logos are placed in the top of the placard: "Supermarkets waste twenty-three million tons of food per year. Go, help yourself!" The poster aims to make the viewer realize the outrageous amount of food destroyed per year by supermarkets and question their right to ownership over the food that is wasted or going to be wasted. According to French law, taking the food in the garbage containers of the supermarket precincts is not an illegal act (*France* Bleu 2018). However, supermarket owners may threaten to sue people who do it, as it often entails breaking-in. The poster may enable students to consider the relationship between property and power, between legality and legitimacy when it comes to obtaining and consuming food: in other words, the canteen is not only a space to satisfy hungry students' basic needs but is also constructed to allow reflecting upon the broader politics of food.

Voices in *A Freedom Factory*, a Promotional Publication by LAP

The voices forming the promotional book *Une Fabrique de Libertés* (A Freedom Factory), published by the LAP community in 2012, encompass voices current and former students and teachers. The authors explore the particular interplay between freedom and obligations in LAP, and the relationship between the pedagogical practices in LAP and the State institutional logic they are caught in, mostly exemplified by the *baccalauréat*. The analysis of the voices in this promotional book will allow for triangulation with the issues identified in the analysis of actual practices above.

As it is part of the State educational system, one of the official objectives of LAP is to prepare their students for taking the *baccalauréat*, or *bac*, the French school-leaving exam. In practice, this means that the official curriculum required to pass the *baccalauréat* will have to be taught in LAP. That is, no matter how alternative the school is, this means that by the end of their education, their activities will be measured by the national standards. Students are expected to pass the preliminary examinations in French at the end of their second year, and all the other subjects at the end of their third year, that is, at the end of their career in secondary school. The *baccalauréat* is, according to the (teachers) authors of *Une Fabrique de Libertés*, reported to be one of the main instrumental purposes of the students when they imagine going to high school: "Students arriving in the class of *seconde* (the first year of high school) are often in great difficulty, and yet consider this first year as 'useless' ", according to these students, "real learning would only start the year after, when preparing for the first part of the *baccalauréat* exam" (Lycée Autogéré de Paris 2012, p. 42). The authors criticize this understanding arguing that this "attitude" has to be fought against because it "pushes back in time the moment when students will start learning" and may lead to their "failure" at the exam. Instead, the document argues that the first year of high school, the so-called *seconde* year requires students to learn regularly and give value to their activities. To this end, they propose a school-made "diploma allowing a positive and concrete self-evaluation".

Further, Eric, a teacher in LAP, reports that he understands the justifications by students who claim that "there is not just the 'bac' " as "coherent justifications" (Lycée Autogéré de Paris 2012, p. 224). He shows how, although he initially disagreed with such an approach, he developed solidarity with the student's voice the further he got involved in LAP. Although the diploma was a "stupid" thing and although he "was trapped with this goal", Eric saw his role as facilitating the students to obtain it to avoid being handicapped in their future in case they lack it. His opinion has changed, and he argues that "today, it is sometimes the opposite, I believe I am relieved to hear from a student that he or she doesn't have the baccalauréat as a goal anymore" (ibid.). Leaving this "normative race towards a certain failure" enable students having other goals to blossom at school (ibid.). If it does not only consist in the instrumental purpose of obtaining the *baccalauréat*, "what is the purpose of LAP then?" asks Eric. Identifying with the voice of LAP, he opens the meaning possibilities of secondary education away from the instrumental diploma:

> The purpose is everything else! To be at school at the same age as one's friends, to be integrated into one's friends group, to have a status in one's family, to have a student card, to grow up as a teenager or young adult, to meet academic knowledge in class, to live in cultural places, to exchange, to work in groups, to learn to use arguments, to get involved in workshops, projects, to participate in a self-managed adventure, to take decisions and to live the limits and the success of this collective project. (ibid.)

Apart from being free to choose whether they want to organize their time in LAP around the *baccalauréat*, students are also free to attend school. In the book, this 'freedom of attendance' exemplifies political freedom, against which many criticisms are generally raised by the upholders of narrow definitions of pedagogical practice and of authoritarian ideologies. Students will be able to, as a result of their 'freedom of attendance', decide what kind of pedagogical practices make sense to them, according to their interests. They will be able to explore a broader range of interests involving different responsibilities than an imposed instrumentality of adaptation to the needs of the labor market. According to the authors, such critics are "manifold" and often distrust or mock at the freedom to attend school, qualifying it as "being too soft with the students", "being unable to get students to respect teachers", or "fostering an anarchist hotbed" (ibid., p. 10). In these terms, the idea of discipline comes to be contested and focuses on the rights and obligations between the individual and the collective. The authors disidentify with the dominant practice of "rules of procedure" that resembles a "penal code". In contrast, in LAP, they gave the institution of "agreement" (*engagement*), that students are obliged to read and sign as a condition for them to begin their school year. The agreement is a declaration of "rights and obligations", elaborated by the whole LAP community, aiming to "resembling the principles that are at the base of life in a society". LAP's assumption of what "life in society" means is thus implied to deny the appropriateness of authoritarian measures of rules and punishments; instead, life in society is about respecting collectively built rights and obligations. The freedom of attendance is positively evaluated, as it represents one of the crucial dimensions of the school. Students "will be able to develop and affirm their personality", "will avoid suffering from schooling" as they "will know how to emancipate themselves from constraints". The modal auxiliaries "will be able to" and "will know how to" evaluate the empowering potential of the practice in LAP.

Constraints to freedom of attendance are associated with the requirement of "pursuing the *baccalauréat*" (Lycée Autogéré de Paris 2012, p. 61). Although it is not an obligation, passing the *baccalauréat* may end up defining, indirectly, the different forms that freedom of attendance can take. For students whose aim is to obtain the certificate, freedom of attendance will be limited to whatever lies 'outside' of the content of the final exam, while subjects required to pass the exam will be chosen by default. Democratic participation in the school functioning leaves the *baccalauréat* issue, which is the condition of survival of the school, beyond democratic reach. Allowing the choice in what to learn and what for, freedom of attendance will also make students accountable for their learning practices. Freedom of attendance allows the students to ask questions, and to be part of a collective; it is not reduced to liberating the individual only (ibid.). Education as an individual constraint is negatively evaluated here, as opposed to education as a practice of collective freedom. Freedom of attendance reinforces the link between the teachers and the students, focusing on help rather than on authority, that is, on the "weapon of punishment" (ibid., p. 22). Freedom of attendance doesn't mean "liberty to do nothing", and while absenteeism in class "will always be the object of a discussion" (ibid., 61), repeated absenteeism in collective duties is evaluated as relatively more undesirable. It may end up being equated with "not belonging to the school anymore" (ibid., p. 136) and it may result, in extreme cases, in an actual punishment: the "deregistration" from the school (ibid.).

For the authors of the book, the development of freedom is allowed by democratic practices, that is by the "collective participation of school members to the process of decision-making" based on the rule of "one person equals one vote" (Lycée Autogéré de Paris 2012, p. 22). Self-management allows learning citizenship in a small collective. The practices of self-management and citizenship are linked because the citizen, according to LAP, is only a citizen in relation to a collective body in which he or she can take common decision based on the recognition of the particular interests of the group. Self-management "contributes" to build interpersonal relations, to "build networks of obligation, exchange and solidarity" (ibid.). In other words, the authors of the document see practices of citizenship-building practices based on "power with". Such practices allow for a democratic form of government since everyone in the school is equal before, and can participate in decision-making processes on any area of school life.

Self-management and democratic participation of all the actors involved in the school are the distinctive features of LAP. Freedom of decision for all the students is "beneficial" to the quality of all the activities offered in LAP. The authors of the promotional book formulate their goals in the form of questions:

> After so many years, the questions remain the same. How do the teachers succeed in managing the place collectively? How are students associated [with teachers] in the management of the school? How to offer them time to stabilize themselves, to find their way and to be able to make their own choices? How to learn while creating freedom for each student and all of them at the same time? (Lycée Autogéré de Paris 2012, p. 18)

These questions reveal the desirable relationship between the individual and the collective and between teachers and students. Teachers are expected to manage the place on an equal footing with students, associated as a collective, and to be teaching the students how to do so. At the same time, teachers are there for students to be able to be free to make their own choices, to develop their personality but also find their place in a democratic collective through which they participate in pedagogical practices allowing them to learn the interrelation between individual freedom and collective freedom. For Paulo Freire (2014, Ch. 4), finding the balance between individual freedom and collective freedom, and between freedom and authority, is one of the main goals of critical pedagogy.

The particular obligations in LAP, its regulative pedagogic discourse, are encoded by means of deontic modality. In the book *Une Fabrique de Libertés*, teachers argue that "every person who becomes a LAP member has to know that he or she will have to actively participate in the 'democratic' life of the school" (Lycée Autogéré de Paris 2012, p. 193), and that "there is a 'moral' obligation to think, to discuss, to deliberate, to put all the knowledge, belonging to any group, in common" (ibid.). The emphasis on supporting students to encourage their self-confidence is also illustrated in Anne-Marie's assertion about her photography workshop: "We have to support students who believe all their pictures are bad and who do not want to show any" by "selecting a few engaging pictures we believe deserve to be exhibited" (ibid., 101). Supporting "self-confidence and confidence in others" is desirable in an instrumental perspective as it "helps students to overcome the fear of other situations, for example, to take the *baccalauréat*" (ibid., p. 102).

SUMMARIZING THE POWER DIALECTICS

The discussion of these different sets of data foregrounded the issue of trust between students and teachers. Because of their position in the educational system, teachers are the ones empowered to take part in the negotiations with the State authorities. In the particular conflict with the Paris academy, teachers considered themselves as the agents embodying the school and the students as a group of people to whom they have to explain what is in their best interest. The asymmetrical relation of 'power against' between the teachers and the students in this particular case was illustrated by the comic book, which could be interpreted as a patronizing device vis-à-vis the students who could not be included in the negotiations. The unequal power relation between teachers and students is also illustrated by the attribute 'subversive', given by some teachers to the students whose way of acting in the decision-making processes of the school is deemed inappropriate. The discussion determined that, similarly to the general assemblies, the passivity of students is taken for granted in most decision-making processes, which leads students to express themselves more freely in other spaces of the school, such as the common areas, or in specific pedagogical activities like classes.

The instrumental purpose of the *baccalauréat* is represented in the book as the main goal of students in LAP, even if for some students, going to secondary school is not about obtaining the diploma. This instrumental purpose is limiting the educational freedom in LAP, not only because preparing for the *baccalauréat* is one of the conditions for the material survival of the school but also because the scope of freedom of attendance can be limited by an instrumental approach to education. Authority is argued to be collective: the injunction to respect rights and obligations that are the outcome of collective processes of decision making. However, if the voices articulated in the promotional book emphasize LAP practices as 'a Freedom Factory', the description of self-management practices by its authors silence the particular configurations of the student/teacher divide in these demonstrated above, and the implications in terms of trust and 'power with'/'power against' relations.

References

France Bleu. 2018. Récupérer de La Nourriture Dans La Poubelle d'un Supermarché n'est Pas Un Délit, 4 December 2018, sec. Infos. https://www.francebleu.fr/infos/societe/recuperer-de-la-nourriture-dans-la-poubelle-d-un-supermarche-n-est-pas-un-delit-1543937451.

Ferri, Jean-Yves, and Manu Larcenet. 2005. *Le retour à la terre, 1: La vraie vie*. Paris: Dargaud.

Freire, Paulo. 2014. *Pedagogy of hope: Reliving pedagogy of the oppressed*. London, New York: Bloomsbury Academic.

Lycée Autogéré de Paris. 2012. *Une Fabrique de Libertés: Le Lycée Autogéré de Paris*. Paris: Editions REPAS.

———. 2020a. RDV Au Rectorat JOUR J, H - 6. 6 May 2020. https://lutteslap.blogspot.com/2020/05/rdv-au-rectorat-jour-j-h-6.html. Accessed 30 Sept 2023.

———. 2020b. Affaire à Suivre... 8 May 2020. https://lutteslap.blogspot.com/2020/05/affaire-suivre.html. Accessed 30 Sept 2023.

———. 2020c. Retour Au Rectorat, Épisode 7 à Suivre... 10 May 2020. https://lutteslap.blogspot.com/2020/05/retour-au-rectorat-episode-7-suivre.html. Accessed 30 Sept 2023.

———. 2020d. Communiqué de Presse Du 12 Mai 2020. *Communiqué de Presse Du 12 Mai 2020* (blog). 12 May 2020. https://lutteslap.blogspot.com/2020/05/communique-de-presse-du-12-mai-2020.html. Accessed 30 Sept 2023.

Pinto, Derrin. 2004. Indoctrinating the youth of post-war Spain: A discourse analysis of a fascist civics textbook. *Discourse and Society* 15 (5): 649–667.

CHAPTER 4

'Radio LAP': Recontextualizing Social Issues in a Transdisciplinary Critical Pedagogic Event

Abstract This chapter presents the analysis of particular 'Radio LAP' pedagogical events. Radio LAP is a 90-minute-long radio program broadcast on *Radio Libertaire*, the self-managed radio of the French Anarchist Federation going on air at 6 pm every two weeks on Thursday. This program's creation is a transdisciplinary activity in which students from any age group can voluntarily enroll in for the whole school year. The topics dealt with in the show are issues of concern for the students, who also share news about their daily educational practices in LAP. The discussion of this activity is going to facilitate the reader's understanding of the recontextualization of different discourses in a potentially critical media discourse. It is recognized by LAP as a pedagogical event as it is one of the available 'projects' for the students (taking place every Thursday afternoon). In short, participation in running the radio is seen as a pedagogical event that allows students to make full use of their creativity and freedom in the production and organization of the weekly programs.

Keywords Critical media studies • Critical discourse analysis • Microethnography • Interdiscursivity • Evaluation

Radio LAP is a 90-minute-long radio program broadcast on *Radio Libertaire*, the self-managed radio of the French Anarchist Federation

© The Author(s), under exclusive license to Springer Nature Switzerland AG 2024
M. Galiere, *Realities of Critical Pedagogy*, Anthropological Studies of Education, https://doi.org/10.1007/978-3-031-40266-1_4

going on air at 6 pm every two weeks on Thursday. Radio Libertaire is broadcast on the local FM band, on the 89.4 MHz frequency and it is also available through online streaming in the whole world since 2004. The radio program came about in September 2011, as part of the available projects in LAP. This program's creation is a transdisciplinary activity in which students from any age group can voluntarily enroll in for the whole school year. The topics dealt with in the show are issues of concern for the students, who also share news about their daily educational practices in LAP. The topics of the programs are decided every three months during a discussion involving the students. Every broadcast consists of a live debate and live presentations by students, punctuated by musical breaks and recordings to be commented during the debates. The Radio LAP group consists of around ten students, and for every broadcast, two students volunteer to be in the control room. The teacher who created the Radio project and who is still in charge, Perrine, is the one responsible for the access to the studio as she is the one who is given its key by the broader radio community.

Analyzing the interactional dynamics of Radio LAP will provide an understanding of the recontextualization of different discourses in a potentially critical media discourse. I chose to divide my analysis into main thematic areas attended to in the Radio shows produced and aired that I could observe during the first semester of the 2019/2020 academic year. First, I will analyze discourses related to the new education policies and their economic context, and second, I will focus on discourses around LGBTQI+ matters.

Situating the Student Protest in the Neoliberal Economy

Education policies and neoliberalism were the main topics of the radio events that took place on 14 November and on 12 December 2019. The November program dealt with education in general while the December program focused on the struggles taking place in universities. One of the issues discussed in the 14 November program is the dramatic incident of the self-immolation of a student named Anas K. in protest against student poverty in the city of Lyon (Chrisafis 2018; Willsher 2019). In the analysis of the transcribed data, I will seek to discern the different actors' commitments to education and their views presented on its economic context pushed to the center of their attention by the shocking student protest in Lyon through an analysis of the participants' evaluative statements made as the radio event was unfolding. The choice of the analytical categories are adopted from Fairclough (2003), who argues "what people commit themselves to in texts is an important part of how they identify themselves, the texturing of identities" (Fairclough 2003, p. 164). He sees modality and evaluation analysis as a way to grasp the value commitments of the speakers with "respect to what is necessary (modality) and with respect to what is desirable or undesirable, good or bad (evaluation)" (ibid.) in their view.

The discussion of the event is bound to recontextualize the 'institutional' or 'official' discourse of the French government and higher education institutions in the program. The policies discussed were focused on the issue of the new *baccalauréat* reform and its relation with the broader inequalities in education. Sam, a student, in the above quote using free indirect speech, reports the actual educational policies of funding that will bring in the hegemonic discourse of the State: "one does not hire tenure teachers anymore because it is too expensive according to the start-up nation". Here, the "start-up nation" refers to the current representation of society held by the government of Emmanuel Macron, who claimed in the early days of his presidency that the French society is composed of "individual entrepreneurs" forming a "start-up nation" (La Croix 2017). In this quote, indirectly attributed to Emmanuel Macron and its government ('according to the start-up nation'), through the grammatical means of free indirect speech, the governmental voice is implicated to evaluate negatively the practice of hiring public servants as a costly measure for the state, a truth that Sam challenges. He explicitly voices his critique when considering it "problematic", since in his evaluation the cut on public spending means that the state increasingly resorts to "massively hiring temporary teachers" who will give "more classes than they should", which in turn creates more "money issues and insecurities"—though not directly for the government but for students and teachers.

Perrine, the teacher, follows by reporting the student demonstrations that were taking place around the time of airing through the verbatim reporting of the voice of the students demonstrating in front of the regional centres of student social services: "What is going on, you have to stop!" However, the very activities that need to be stopped, that is, the government's austerity measures are not named. Sam's response highlights the effects of the government's overall austerity politics for students' life through proposing an actual solution for students instead of the government's program: "in the student demands; we could have the idea of a student salary". Sam identifies with the students' voice "we" and commits himself in the collective of this 'we' to demand a "student salary" as a desirable objective that is at the same time modalized "we could have", indicating that this is in fact not a demand but a proposal for discussion.

What I have shown through the analysis of the exchange between Sam and Perrine is the working of interdiscursivity through the systemic use of different forms of reporting that at the same time also implicates different forms of speaker positioning in relation to the actors represented in the sentences. These linguistic devices work together to do the textual work of "accentuation of difference, conflict, polemic, a struggle over meaning, norms, and power" (Fairclough 2003, p. 42) between the distanced representation of the government's voice and the radio show participants' critical stance of what they see as austerity measures imposed upon the already dispossessed in the name of an alleged 'solution' and by extension between a neoliberal representation of the role of the state in the political economy in relation to public spending, and a radical democratic representation in the student voice that is in explicit conflict with such a representation, arguing for more targeted public spending but in a modalized statement, keeping the space open to debate a solution represented from the position of the dispossessed already struck by social problems facing higher education, such as generalized insecurity (Barot 2010).

The modalization is made more visible in the face of the actual Lyon event. The suicide by self-immolation of Anas K. in Lyon has pushed the polemic dimension of the situation to an extreme. He left a letter on Facebook to explain his gesture. A part of this letter, representing the level of precarity, is directly reported by Laurent, a student, in the radio event: "this year is my third attempt to validate my second BA year, I did not receive a grant. Before that, when I had a grant, it was 450 euros a month. Is that enough to live?" Direct reporting of this part of the letter over indirect reporting of its gist produces the effect of acknowledging the heroism of Anas K.'s action as well as its validity in the face of the government's killing austerity measures. Anas K.'s voice, therefore, indirectly comes to be recognized as more authoritative than the government's voice in representing the effects of austerity in public spending—this way working as the ultimate authority supporting the suggestion of introducing a student wage. Seen from this perspective, the use of modalization in "We could have a student wage" is not functioning to reduce the seriousness of students demands, including Anas K.'s public sacrifice, but can be seen as an invitation addressed to the sympathetic listener of the program, inviting them to come up with other options.

Other instances of conflicting discourses emerge and accentuate explicitly the tensions between representations of the subject of education as an isolated individual, which is the material realities of education in France, and representations of the subject of education as part of a broader collective uniting their power to challenge that individualized figure of the student, which is inherently a depoliticized and depoliticizing act on behalf of the neoliberal management of social conflicts. The hegemonic discourse of individual responsibility is reported by Sam: "a lot of people say that you have to find the required resources to succeed". In this sentence, "you have to" is an instance of deontic modality: it is a strong obligation, a requirement implicating the imposition of this victimization that blames the individual for their fate on the subject by the eternal world (a lot of people in agreement with the government)—while 'must' would indicate the speaker's identification with and internalization of the obligation (Fairclough 2003, p. 170).

Sam continues then to counter this imposition of obligation explicitly entering into an imaginary debate with the 'lot of people' by exposing the imposition's contradictory nature: "try to work while studying for a degree and try to finish your studies properly". At the same time, the reality of this contradiction is mitigated by the use of a low degree of epistemic modality of the expression that is meant to support the validity of the student's position: instead of providing actual statistical figures, he simply appeals to an expected shared experience of the listeners when saying his claim stands "in the majority of cases". But if we understand this specific radio program to be contextualized in many other programs, discussing the effects of the austerity measures, the "majority of cases" can be seen as an indirect reference to them, positing the listener as a 'regular audience member' of the weekly LAP programs. In fact, in a radio event in my data I recorded on 12 December, Patricia, another LAP student, reports a comparable event informed by the hegemonic neoliberal discourse of individual responsibility and obligation: "I feel that society is telling me that as a student, you have to go find a student job; otherwise you will never learn to manage your own life". And adds that "it is clearly impossible to live in Paris while only earning 450 euros per month". Exposing the detrimental effects of the lack of public funding in education.

The contribution of Perrine, the teacher, is to reinforce the validity of the student's generalization (in the majority of cases) by exposing the class ideology at work performed by the strategic individualization. In that same program, she reports the general aspects of the individualizing discourse by direct reporting that is to discredit the actors named: "they talk about success, about the ability to motivate oneself, to be creative" but it works only for a particular social group of society:

> You have to belong to the right social group, when you speak about success, about being able to be motivated, to be creative, it's not given to everyone, it conceals inequalities that exist and that are reinforced, even more than before … it reminds me of the 'free choice' curriculum, that is what we do in LAP but in our case it is very different it can mean not taking the baccalauréat, look at Clem he will create his permaculture structure for instance.

According to Perrine, the individualization in fact universalizes the privileges of a particular social group, hiding existing inequalities, and she argues that individualizing discourse has hijacked the idea of 'free choice' in which she identifies a democratic potential when applied in LAP. She chooses to modalize "free choice" as allowing for different meanings since it can mean choosing not to take the *baccalauréat* exam, or to strive toward any life goal as it can also mean being free to choose to set up a permaculture structure. Conversely, individualizing discourse reduces freedom of choice to choose how to achieve better the consensual yet class-specific norm of "individual success". For PG, freedom of choice turns into an obligation to choose "already before you enter high school [at the age of 15] you will have to think about what to do after the baccalauréat exam". Facing this obligation, not everyone is positioned equally: those "whose family will grasp all this" will be rewarded with "success", that is, able to meet the new measures of graduation from high school. In contrast, for the "others" this obligation will turn into a different one, a matter of economic survival that gets in the way of their school performance: "they will have to go to work" instead.

In the specific radio event of Radio LAP aired on 14 November 2019, I analyze how the democratic practice of free choice in the LAP education comes to be recontextualized as an act of opening a dialogue about how to understand the social issue discussed, that is, student austerity and its impact on self-governing educational institutions like LAP. At the same time, the hegemonic discourse of neoliberal precarity is seen as suppressing "differences of meaning and norms" to reach a "consensus" that will normalize asymmetries of power (Fairclough 2003, p. 42). I argue that drawing on Perrine's reflections, this logic also results in naturalizing the commodification of 'educational success', the classist effect of austerity measures. The debate in the radio program has underscored a connection between the neoliberal ideology of equality of opportunity and the reproduction of social inequalities in education policies: the ideological meaning of 'freedom of choice' is very different from that of the LAP practices enabling the students in the radio program to expose that ideology at work is the new measures of the French government. Their legitimization functions as a way of representing the inequalities in the socio-economic situations of individuals as a result of their responsibility for making the choices as if unconditionally available, that will yield the best "return of investment" when the opportunities arise (Brown 2015, p. 178).

In addition to a selective use of reporting speech and modality, I could also identify the extensive use of irony in the radio programs, especially when Patricia was on air. It is another effective linguistic device to produce conflicting dialogizations of the neoliberal discourse on education. In the program aired on 14 November, Patricia ironizes, "Come on, you have to be transversal", "You did not validate your transversal skill, your flexibility isn't the best". These are instances where she intends to mimic the constraining dimension of the dominant discourse. "You have to be" associated with the attribute "transversal", which seems bizarre here as it is generally used in the phrase 'transversal skills' in the dominant discourse (Laval et al. 2011, p. 96) rather than to qualify human beings. In the second sentence, the disciplinary aspect of the dominant discourse is mimicked, and although "transversal" is used in its conventional form as an attribute of skill, the ironic dimension resides in the potentially polysemic meaning of "flexible" when qualifying a human being. At another point, Patricia designs a sentence illustrating an ideal rationalization of subjectivity according to the neoliberal logic: "My personal project is to get motivated to make money, and if I manage then it will be a success". The irony resides in the bizarre lining up of the managerial terms "personal project", "motivation", "money-making" and "success" in one single sentence. In "I am in favor of failing", the positive evaluation of "failure", an extremely negative term in the neoliberal discourse, does not only intend to expose the potentially ideological meaning of the word but also of its antonym "success".

Eddy, a student, positions herself in the debate as someone in total disagreement with the new *baccalauréat* reform: "I am totally against new *baccalauréat* reform". In Eddy's opinion, the so-called reform is in fact a political act of foreclosing an "egalitarian education". Education is implicitly evaluated as desirable if it is egalitarian. The *baccalauréat* exam, whether new or old, is generally evaluated as undesirable, the "new" and "old *baccalauréat*" being two evils: "people who are generally against the *baccalauréat* are forced to fight for the old *baccalauréat*, to choose the lesser evil". He further adds that he doesn't "feel like fighting alongside reactionaries against the reform", foregrounding the positive evaluation of this 'non-reactionary' identity, since being identified as a reactionary is undesirable. The fact that the *baccalauréat* reform coincides with other new laws he represents as "attacks", and as such, they are evaluated as "dangerous" because they are seen to "weaken the strength" of the social movement by accentuating the divisions amongst students who should form a collective of solidarity. The desirability of unity in the struggles against government policies and for social justice is recurrent in the Radio LAP events. For instance, Patricia, in the radio program aired on 12 December, produces a positive evaluation of the unity she has witnessed in the ongoing strikes against the pension reforms that is produced by her choice of an affective mental process verb: "I *liked* that the strikes were not only centered on the pensions issues but centered on both education AND pensions".

Patricia, in comparison with the other participants in the programs, is a student who uses a more informal way of conveying evaluations as part of her identity. Its effect is to break the media discourse norm of formality, attract more attention to her words or reduce the social distance between herself and the potential listeners and her classmates. She argues that higher education is "a shitty system" that is "screwed up" (*il y a des petites couilles*) because of "private journals", "privatized research", "buying information" and making researchers "pay to be able to do research"), in which the state doesn't do much apart from creating "shitty jobs". She makes an association between precariousness, the commodification and the privatization of education to reject it in the next sentence as "a catastrophe". S, another student, is concerned by the substitution of "public interests" by "private interests" at the level of higher education. He claims that "making money with research" is a "big problem" causing "great worries" about the transformation of the French system into an "Americanized" one. "*A l'Américaine*" indirectly refers to the economic dimension of higher education in the United States, an implicit negative marker that remains without a detailed explanation.

In this section, I have shown that the voice of the government is brought into a polemic dialogue by the students in the programs of Radio LAP. Several hegemonic discourses on education and its economic context were dialogized for critique during the Radio LAP event concerning the developments of the struggles in higher education against the latest governmental reforms. The main issues that are polemicized are neoliberal austerity policies and the individualization of students in the education system that only reproduces social inequalities. The various linguistic means of dialogicity, that is, the accentuation of difference and the focus on solidarity, are used to articulate a counter-hegemonic stance aiming at responding to the suppression of social differences as if non-existent. Polemicizing the hegemonic discourse in education by exposing some of its absurdities was also shown to be achieved through the use of irony. Identities of the speakers were negotiated through evaluations and modalizations while collective knowledge and action were framed as desirable. In contrast, the implications of governmental reforms were framed as undesirable represented as ideological tools to naturalize and make privatization in education a desirable means for 'success'.

GENDER AND LGBTQI+ ISSUES

Gender and LGBTQI+ matters are raised in my data of the Radio LAP programs on 26 September and 14 November 2019. On 26 September, the actual event discussed was concerned with the *Pride Banlieues* (Suburban Pride) that had taken place on 9 June 2019 in the Paris suburb of Saint-Denis ('Marche des fiertés à Saint-Denis: "La banlieue aussi a une vie queer"' 2019). In the other program aired on 14 November, Eddy, a student, defining her identity as a transgender girl, made a presentation about the ExistransInter, a march for the defense of Trans and Intersex rights ('Cinq choses à savoir sur "ExisTransInter", la marche des personnes trans et intersexes ce week-end' 2019). Some students from LAP had taken part in the Pride Banlieues and the ExistransInter marches. Other topics concerning gender were the question of gender-based violence such as rape, femicides and the #metoo movement, discussed during the program aired on 26 September.

Ahmed, one of the LAP students who participated in the pride banlieue, reports the voice of "ordinary people" to link the commonsense representation about the suburbs with that of the mainstream media representations of these areas, constructing a belief among "ordinary people" that "we cannot be queer in the suburbs". This representation is polemicized in the Radio LAP event: "When we were talking about the Pride Banlieues in the media, we ended up talking about Islam or theology [...] the main fear people had about the pride was to see hordes of jihadists armed with Kalashnikovs, guns, burning everybody down", says Ahmed. He attributes to the mainstream media the ideology representing French suburbs as a hotbed of Islam and Islamic extremism, in which intolerance against gays can lead to terrorist attacks. This is an ideology of denationalization of violence that has the effect of representing Islam as foreign to French identity (Delphy 2015, 'Extraordinary Violence'), silencing the fact that homophobic violence is independent of race and is found across the whole French society. Ahmed was "surprised" that "this fear came up to be represented as well-founded" and that in the end, "obviously", "nothing like that happened". Ahmed then foregrounds the hegemonic discourse of the "legitimate national identity" without attributing to anyone in particular and adds "homosexual norms have been integrated to [it]". He polemicizes the homosexual identity elevated to a norm by this discourse is a "Parisian, white, male, rich and now married, gay person", and that according to her, this translates into the "stigmatization" of homosexuals who do not fit in this norm, "that is to say, Muslims". According to this, the hegemonic discourse on national identity tends toward the extreme right and turns into a justification of xenophobic agendas: Ahmed reports that "we hear European extreme-right leaders say" that "we should be stopping immigration immediately", because "Muslims do not like homosexuals" and "we like homosexuals"; to what Ahmed answers, exposing the ideological implication of extreme-right discourse: "as if immigration only concerned Muslims", a suggestion she calls "grotesque". The Pride Banlieue is an action that can challenge the hegemonic discourse in which tolerance with a certain kind of people serves as a justification to the oppression of others, by connecting the struggles in an intersectional way. The teacher present in the event, Perrine, reports the voice of the Pride Banlieue participants and organizers she read in an article: "you are denouncing police violence, or more all-encompassing issues like housing problems", that leads her to conclude that "you do not create a hierarchy among the different struggles", "therefore it allows you to be able to fight on many different grounds at the same time", which is all evaluated in "I think this all is pretty positive". She contrasts this intersectional discourse a discourse generally attributed to leftist movements thus framed negatively, which fetishizes and empties the notion of "revolution" of its meaning: "we often say okay, we have to think about all this, but we will see after the revolution". In the same way, Eddy, a student, generally reports what Prides "revendicated in history", and often do not in the present: "communist, anarchist, alter-globalist and often antiracist revendications", whereas now they end with a "speech from the mayor" and her "ultra-dangerous liberal discourse" on "personal identities when it is actually a collective struggle". She sees the Pride Banlieue as the legitimate heir of the historical Prides. In another program that was aired on 14 November, Eddy also sees the ExistransInter march as an heir of the politicized Prides, directly quoting the march's motto: "mutilated, deported, assassinated", written in "gender-neutral language" [*Mutilé·es, expulsé·es, assassiné·es*] as a way to encompass different categories of oppressed trans people, for instance, migrant trans people "often deported" and "racialized", "ending up being the first victims of transphobic aggressions or assassinations". Dialogicity the Pride Banlieue and the ExistransInter focuses on "commonality" and "solidarity" (Fairclough 2003, p. 42) with their demands.

Aside from the dialogized voices that are either evaluated negatively or positively through polemic or solidarity, several other instances of evaluation occurred during the event. I will show what the participants framed as desirable and undesirable through evaluative statements. For example, "Prides" without a "political dimension" are "incoherent" according to Ahmed, for whom the "systemic racism" via the "fetishization of racial identity" in the "LGBTQI+ community in Paris" representing racialized (Arab) homosexuals as " 'Scheherazade' out for a good time" is also something "that cannot be let happen anymore". Eddy, taking the identity of the invisible ("me, as a trans woman, who did not feel represented"), adds that in "traditional Prides" in "trans and intersex causes" are "invisible", bringing about a negative evaluation of mainstream "Prides" as exclusionary. Ahmed draws a parallel between white masculinity and violence against oppressed minorities through a reference to the institution of the police: "In the bus [back from the pride] we were the victims of police violence, we had this moment of display of masculinity that we enjoy so much, what's more of white masculinity (laughs)". Ahmed rejects verbal violence as well when he calls the use of the term "hermaphrodite" to depict intersexual people as one to "be avoided". Concerning the Pride Banlieue, the solidarity demonstrated by non-queer immigrants "because they just wanted to see something change positively in their suburb" is welcomed by Ahmed who qualifies that of "really cool". In contrast, criticism from "white gays" of "caucus spaces for women" and of a "women-only procession" leading to the cancellation of the latter is evaluated through the mental process, expressed in local slang, "it disgusted me" (*ça m'a fané*). Caroline values positively the intersectionality of the Pride Banlieue: "it did me so much good" to hear that there is a "Pride that we have been waiting for so long", which is "politicized, intersectional and representative", that incorporates "current matters like undocumented migration, police violence", and that "this incredible Pride [...] takes place [...] and is organized in the suburbs". Eddy relates the ExistransInter march to its legislative context: the amendments presented to the bioethics law that was voted in the same period were rejected. These "affect the lives of intersexual persons": "one amendment was about forbidding surgeries on intersexual people at birth, without their consent" which entails the act of "forcing people into boxes at birth, which is medically unnecessary". Another amendment "aimed at extending the right to assisted reproductive technologies to transgender people", a domain in which "France is late, even compared to her immediate neighbors", while one more amendment proposed "the deletion of the notion of gender in the civil status, which would solve quite a lot of problems" because "it is absolutely useless to do so". Thus, forcing the removal of intersexual people at birth, denying reproductive rights to transgender people and forcing people in gendered boxes are framed as oppressive, undesirable actions. The rejection of the amendments makes Eddy ask the question of the influence some right-wings may have on the government: "We can see that the government gives in to transphobic and reactionary movements", for example, "La Manif pour Tous" [*Demonstrating is for Everyone*, an anti-same-sex marriage organization] and "Marchons Enfants" [*Let's go Children*, an offspring of the Manif pour Tous specifically concerned about the struggle against assisted reproductive technologies] ('La Manif pour tous' 2020). Another student, Laurent, emphasizes that "there were a lot of fascist groups in the Manif pour Tous march, such as Génération Identitaire [Identitarians] or Cocarde Etudiante", drawing a parallel link between intolerant right-wing groups and government policy.

The desirability of the Prides' intersectional aspects is also encoded through the use of modality. Ahmed argues that "sexual, environmental, migratory or whatever matters should not be excluded" by the Pride. Moreover, the prevalence of individualizing approaches to LGBTQI+

matters "should not happen". The Pride "should be anticapitalistic, feminist and ecologist". Eddy adds that people whose voices are excluded from the media "should be" on the foreground instead of the Mayor of Paris when it comes to speaking about LGBTQI+ questions. She also uses modality to encode the undesirability of individualizing approaches to gendered violence, more specifically femicides, and to push for a broader analysis of its social conditions: "the lexical field used [in the dominant discourse] to qualify these assassinations might seem innocent, but femicides by a partner or ex-partner are a social fact that must be considered as a whole as a symptom of the patriarchal system". Arguing that "the whole system has to be indicted", Eddy calls for the desirability of what she considers part of a solution: "denouncing" the system as a whole, and of "funding" to better "avoid dangerous situations". Also, the government's responsibility "should be exposed" and a "restless, ruthless mobilization should be organized".

The issue of gender relations and gendered violence was also an important theme recurring in the Radio LAP programs. In the particular program that I singled out for my analysis was aired on 26 September, voices of victims of gendered violence are introduced by Perrine, the teacher, and Yoann, a student, as "accounts on social networks" of "people who said, this happened to me", for instance, "a Nigerian actress who spoke up to denounce a sexual aggression from Harvey Weinstein", or "the American actress Alyssa Milano who asked women to tell what they suffered through the #metoo hashtag". Dialogicity focuses on solidarity with the voices of these victims: Yoann argues that it is "very important" that it happened, it had "a positive effect on the consciousness of the population about these facts", "unfortunately not much more than moral postures"; while Perrine understands that "it is extremely difficult to put words on rape and even more to report to the police, as not much is done to help rape victims", implicitly valuing the courage that it takes to speak up. Fabien, a student, recognizes that the definition of "rape" has been opened up thanks to the victims' testimonies: "it is not anymore about backstreet rapes, it opened the question of consent [...] which proves this moment has been of importance". According to the participants in the event, the mainstream media are conveying hegemonic representations of gendered violence, and they dedicated the following part of the event criticizing these. Eddy criticizes the discourse of the mainstream media on gendered violence, indirectly quoting the discourse of a feminist collective: "these militants criticize the traditional media who do not communicate much on the problem or misrepresent it. They denounce the use of terms such as 'crimes of passion' or 'family drama' [by the media] and fight for the use of the word 'femicide' ". These "should be" represented not as "trivial events", "result of the individual passions", but as systemic social facts. For that purpose, the feminist collective wants to use the phrase "patriarchal terrorism". Eddy argues that this expression is justified as religious terrorism is over-represented in the media relative to the victims it generates: "it is a more deadly phenomenon than religious terrorism, but the media won't just speak about it because it does not create as much hype". The dialogical aspects of solidarity with the feminist collective and critique of institutional discourse is emphasized by Eddy: "The collective denounce governmental inaction and calls everyone to call out to the President of the Republic on social networks so that the government acts". The personification of governmental power in France by the president of the Republic is taken for granted here, social networks are seen as a potential facilitator of a direct dialogue between citizens and the president/government.

Eddy polemicizes the government discourse he typically sees as "pretending" to care about "men/women equality" through "mediatic brainwashing", while when it comes to concrete actions, it prioritizes austerity politics, giving "a thousand fewer times the amount of money that the feminist associations are legitimately asking for in to fight against gendered violence". The government also answers by "improving the police service", which Eddy qualifies as "ironic", arguing that the police is one of the institutions of the state in which the "sexist attitudes" are the most prevalent. Another instance of Eddy quoting what the government typically says when it comes to funding a public response to gendered violence is "there is no money". Eddy denies the truth of this argument by comparing the derisory sum of money required by feminist groups to the amount of money given to "antiterrorist policies" and to "making the rich even richer", in total amounting to "dozens of billions of euros". Later in the event, during her presentation of a women's march in the financial district of Johannesburg, South Africa (Francke 2019), a student named Caroline quotes "the demands of the women": "two per cent of all the profits of the stock exchange should go to organizations fighting against gendered violence and fund gendered violence victim support centers", "that all the workers be able to report gendered violence at their workplace to a qualified person", "to have specific public transportation for women working at night" or "programs to help victims of gendered violence". The solidarity Caroline demonstrates in her dialogue with the demands of the South

African feminist organization is a way to emphasize that independently of the country, the feminist struggle is international. Moreover, the emphasis on the stock exchange taxation exposes the fact that sufficient wealth is created, and that the issue lays in its just repartition.

The voice of "antifeminists" is also polemicized and rejected during the event by Yoann, asserting in the name of all the participants: "when we hear antifeminists, people we do not like at all [laughs], say that 'well I have compassion for the rapists or the frotteurs from the metro because they must be in sexual or mental distress' ". The "antifeminists" representation of gendered violence as individual responsibility is rejected, rather, Yoann highlights the systematic aspect of such violence: "I think that these cases aren't the majority, I rather think that this is linked to a feeling of powerfulness, as it is not punished, or very little".

Regarding the question of gendered violence, Eddy qualifies as an "improvement" yet "not a perfect situation" of the Spanish way of protecting women from gendered violence, which consists in "the government giving two hundred million euros to this cause, and setting up special courts for women who are the victim of gendered violence, in which it is not the victim but the state who registers a complaint against the perpetrator". Another student, Mickaël, acknowledges that on the one hand, the Spanish authorities positively use money as it "is used to help" the people concerned by gendered violence, and "do prevention", which is by association evaluated as another desirable action. On the other hand, he contrasts it with a "lack of visibility of this issue" in France. Caroline's opinion concurs with the identified visibility problem, and finds it "important" to foreground the fact that gendered violence also happens in other countries and to "give information about the different forms they can take". She negatively evaluates that "there is no information about South Africa in the traditional media". She finds it desirable, "important", "to tell about the lives of women and gender minorities in South Africa" (see the subchapter on intertextuality above). A book on the topic of rape in an activist community is then presented by Perrine, the teacher, who understands the effort of its authors as "trying not to be too psychologizing" and "Trying to make the problem understood as a structural one rather than as an individual one". Explaining structural problems as caused by the individuals' psychology is framed as undesirable by the authors of the book, and Perrine expresses that she "finds this quite positive". The authors' will to create "intersectional struggles" instead of "prioritizing some struggles over others" through "women-only popular education" is positively evaluated and contrasted with the "male resistance", "strategies to undermine their credibility (*décrédibilisation*)", and the "defamation" that the authors' actions had to face.

The intertextuality analysis of LGBTQI+ and gender-related issues in the events showed that a wide range of intertwined racist, sexist, homophobic and neoliberal hegemonic discourses came to be polemicized. Discourses identified as coming from oppressed sections of society are dialogized with an emphasis on solidarity, such as the ones produced by the Pride Banlieue, ExistransInter, feminist watchdogs or rape victims. Intersectionality in struggles emerged as a desirable value, as well as the representation of the oppressed gendered minorities by themselves. Comparably to the discussion of education analyzed above, strong political will aiming at increasing public funding and redistributing wealth to confront unfair social situations is framed as desirable by the participants. In contrast, the influence of right-wing political groups is represented as hindering any progress in a socially fairer direction.

Migrations, Nuclear Energy and Strikes

The three main themes that were also recorded at length in my data of Radio LAP programs were the issues of migrations, discussed on 28 November 2019; the issue of nuclear energy discussed on 10 October 2019 and the issue of organizing strikes in the context of the struggles around the educational system, on 12 December 2019. The issue of migration and refugees has been a key social problem in France since the nineteenth century (Noiriel 2014), with an increased presence in the mediatic field in the past decade. So the choice of the topic in Radio LAP in itself opens up a space for critical reflections. The program aired on 28 November, with the participation of the students Lorène, Yoann, Eddy and their teacher Perrine, therefore, allows me to explore how critical voices and identities on the topic of migrations come to be articulated in a critical pedagogic event. The program deals with the theme of migration as a matter of the daily life of the refugees in the Porte de la Chapelle refugee camp in Paris. It is situated within a broader explanation of the socio-economic contexts of migration in France. The choice of the topic of nuclear energy also shows a critical sensitivity of the volunteers running the Radio LAP program. Nuclear energy as a topic was aired because some LAP students, in agreement with the democratic and radical principle of the school, participated in the *Vent de Bure* (Bure's wind) on 28 and 29

September 2019 in Nancy, a city in eastern France. The event is called that way because it consists of demonstrations protesting against CIGEO, the Meuse/Haute Marne Underground Research Laboratory, which is responsible for planning the repository of radioactive waste in underground tunnels in Bure, a village near Nancy (Meuse/Haute Marne Underground Research Laboratory 2019). In the case of a nuclear accent, the 'wind' from Bure would carry dangerous radioactive material to the city of Nancy. As I have shown in Chap. 3, when exploring the basic values of LAP in the analysis of the actual assembly meeting, political organizing and planning participation in demonstrations and strikes are integral to everyday school life at LAP; hence, it is also an essential matter in Radio LAP to address those events and contribute to the ongoing debates about their relevance for LAP.

The program discussing migration and refugees was aired on 28 September 2019, the topic of migration and refugees. The dominant approach to migration in France is inextricably linked to the colonial history of the country, the general stance on it represents it either as an 'invasion' or as a way to generate 'economic wealth'. In general, the main group of 'migrants' in every era had been victim of various forms of discriminations in the French society (Noiriel 2014), which is particularly true in the case of the so-called 'post-colonial' immigration, settling in France from the former colonies, from the 'end' of the French colonial empire after World War II up until today (Silverstein 2018). The rejection of this particular type of migration is associated today to a broader rejection of the Islamic religion, since a majority of the subjects of the French colonial empire were Muslims (Delphy 2015).

In the Radio LAP event, the general French ideology on the current migration issues is dialogized to be exposed as xenophobic and repressive. Lorène is a student who was volunteering for an association giving free breakfast to "up to 700" refugees living in the Porte de la Chapelle camp in Paris. She claims that "despite the language barrier, they want to tell you their stories by all possible means", to which Perrine, the teacher, answers that "your experience contrasts with the official voice", with "what can be heard in the media" and with "the xenophobic discourses that can be heard from all sides of the political spectrum". Perrine indirectly associates "xenophobic discourses" to the "official voice" and "the media" without giving specific details of their content, apart from the fact that Lorène's experience with refugees, emphasizing their human dimension, is seen to be in contradiction with these discourses. Further, Perrine reports an official term in an ironic way, "Libya cooperates with European countries to dissuade migrants from crossing the Mediterranean".

The polemic dimension of irony comes from the fact that "cooperation", a positively connoted term in everyday discourse, also encompasses several cases of human rights abuse that were reported by NGOs in Libyan detention camps for refugees, for instance, enslaving (Graham-Harrison 2017). Yoann reports media discourse as well: "in the media, they sometimes say 'there were operations carried out to prevent human trafficking' ", to which he grants some truthfulness "it exists" but still opposes since he doesn't consider criminalizing smugglers as "a solution to the root of the problem", which he doesn't explain in details. Subsequently, Yoann reports dominant media discourse on the left/right divide in politics (see Rimbert and Halimi 2018) in a general way through the existential assumption "there is not anymore the left versus right division [in politics] but the liberals versus nationalists one", and invites other participants to discuss the truth of the assumption: "is there a real difference in how extreme-right approaches like Salvini's and extreme-liberal approaches like Macron's in how migrants are treated?" Although Lorène does not want to claim any knowledge about the truth of the assumption "I do not know although there is, I think, a difference", Perrine argues that she "can assure you" the situation is "worse now", that is, under 'liberal' Emmanuel Macron than it was under "rightist hardliners like [Nicolas] Sarkozy", thus denying the truthfulness of the "liberals versus nationalists" division. Eddy approves Perrine's argument and adds that "liberal ideology tends to become an extreme-right ideology in some aspects". These aspects identified with the extreme right are the national symbols and patriotic values: "when one looks at the Macronist youth movement (*JAM, Jeunes avec Macron*), they identify with patriotic values, the French flag, the European flag".

The discussion of migration led the Radio LAP teacher, Perrine, to evaluate using epistemic modality, that is, modalizing the truth commitment of her evaluation, that "maybe", the "criminalization of humanitarian organizations" hence the "non-respect of international law by the EU" is undesirable as it gives "more room for human traffickers", and that "if the EU respected international law, there wouldn't be all these people" who "make money on the back of refugees, I can imagine". Further on, Yoann also mitigates the truth commitment of his evaluation "I have the feeling that we spend so much money to prevent migrants from coming in" and that "with all that money used to build walls, we could save a lot of people and have a normal situation". Here, preventing "migrants" from entering the country and spending money on border reinforcement is seen by Yoann as a situation that is not "normal". Lorène, who is working for a humanitarian NGO, argues that the existence of humanitarian NGOs is undesirable, through deontic modality "what we do in Paris is called humanitarian action, we deal with 3000 people, it's not so much, but there should not be humanitarian [structures] in France. In 2019, 3000 people represent the size of a traditional high school in Paris". In addition to the evaluation of humanitarian action, being able to help 3000 persons is "not much" compared to the actual needs. Eddy adds that "it is the State who should implement solidarity mechanisms to help people" and that "it is crazy for a government to claim that it is the humanitarian NGO's task to help migrants, rather than the public authority. Eddy argues that the state policy to deport migrants is "purely racist" as it is "free or even expensive to expel them". Deportation is not only undesirable from an antiracist ethical point of view, but also from an economical one, as it is implied that it is not "expensive" nor "free" to keep migrants, that is, it could be profitable since there are "studies that show that welcoming migrants in a country generates a boost in the economy".

The Radio LAP participants in the program also expose the ideological dimension of the law-and-order discourse used by the police during the closing of the Porte de la Chapelle refugee camp. Lorène reports official discourses from the Paris police chief and from the city mayor, the first claiming that "there will not be any more refugee camps in Paris by the end of the year" while the latter arguing that "we are putting them [the refugees] in a safe place where they will be kept warm". Lorène brings to light that although "the police headquarters argue that they did not break up the refugee camp but only did customary street work to shelter the refugees", the police operation ended with "two to three hundred refugees sheltered", which "associations expose as 'underproportioned' since only twenty to thirty per cent of the people were sheltered", while "hundred sixty people were arrested and placed in detention centers".

The program aired on 10 October 2019 recontextualizes several antinuclear demands coming from several activist social movements and organizations like *Vent de Bure* or the Collective Against the Atomic Order (*Collectif Contre l'Ordre Atomique*). Anne-Marie, a member of the Collective Against the Atomic Order, was invited by the Radio LAP participants to participate in the debate. The general arguments attributed to anti-nuclear activists movements are indirectly reported by Eddy: "In anti-nuclear movements, we can find the main demand which is the consulting of citizens, [...] in Vent de Bure I heard 'nuclear energy everywhere, democracy nowhere' ", and somewhat more directly by Perrine, who has "looked at the leaflet [of the Collective Against the Atomic Order] and ... the democracy issue is very important, there has been a lot of silence and propaganda [from the state], while they [the Collective] are trying to provide us with information". Eddy and Perrine consider the democratic dimension of the anti-nuclear demands as the most important one. According to Anne-Marie, the state recuperates the democratic demands while dispossessing the citizens of knowledge and their power of decision, since "they will organize a consultation but decisions are taken somewhere else" and that "consultations are useless unless if citizens have something to say and can participate in the decision-making process". The demands of anti-nuclear movements, specifically Vent de Bure, are argued to be silenced by the mainstream media and to be repressed by the police: Eddy claims that "their method is similar to what was used when they treated the Yellow Vests movement, as a few days before the demonstration a press release [from the police] appears alerting that 'rioters are coming', causing the closure of entire parts of the city". The media, therefore, focuses "on potential violence rather than on the demands of the movement" while the police are deployed in "exceptional proportions". This repressive context leads the anti-nuclear movement to also "demand the right to demonstrate".

The ideological discourse of the nuclear corporations and of the state that supports them is also brought into dialogue in the event: Anne-Marie brings up the early justification of the nuclear industry in "civilian nuclear power has been introduced as a peaceful nuclear power as opposed to the construction of the atomic bomb, which was for the independence of France, right?" She exposes that nuclear power is never peaceful nor solely 'French' because of its context of production that exploits societies and the environment: "for the production of civilian nuclear power, we extract uranium in mines in Niger, Kazakhstan, and Canada, which generates extreme pollution". Anne-Marie more directly quotes the nuclear industry discourse to refute the ideology of development used to justify uranium mining: "in these countries, they were told that mines are 'bringing work, development, etc. it is fantastic' "; however, she criticizes this argument because the "dangers for the surrounding cities are not explained" and "there are almost no financial spinoffs for the local populations". The State Nuclear Safety Authority's (ASN, *Agence de Sûreté du Nucléaire*) discourse is dialogized by Anne-Marie, who emphasizes the commonality with their present discourse while polemicizing what she claims was their discourse in the past "the ASN says that the risk of a nuclear accident is probable" and although they previously "said it was improbable, impossible", "there were three severe accidents".

The program in which nuclear power is discussed is organized by a logic of critical reflection. The perspective of the representation of the demonstration against, and that of the government's plan about the depository of nuclear waste in Bure, is produced by the presenters' claims to the lack of democracy and the lack of information for citizens and these lacks are framed as undesirable by evaluative markers in phrases such as "they are creating citizen consultations that are organized so well that they will never know anything more, such consultations are useless" (Anne-Marie). Eddy brings a negative evaluation of the repressive approach to anti-nuclear demonstrations in "the repression level is alarming", "the police chiefs are lying" and "the police dispositive is absurd". The Vent de Bure demonstration and demonstrators are framed positively by Eddy, who was one of the participants, in the following phrases "it was a lively and radical demonstration", "the demonstration draws a bridge between the antinuclear struggle and the ecological, social and political emergencies" while "not letting repression prevail, nor discourage them". Removed out of democratic reach, the embeddedness of nuclear energy in the logic of privatization and profit-making is evaluated by Eddy in "we were speaking about subcontracting, there is something very alarming, that the subcontracting level is increasing because EDF is less and less profitable. This is extremely dangerous". EDF (Electricité de France), the former state-owned electricity company to which the nuclear infrastructure inside the French borders belongs, is partially privatized since 2004, henceforth functions in a profit-oriented way; this is "alarming" for Eddy, given the dangerousness of nuclear power. Modalized sentences are less present in the event dealing with nuclear energy, the only occurrences of deontic modality are emphasizing Radio LAP participants' duty to provide information and foster action: "what we should know is that if there is a weak link in the steel structure of a reactor, it explodes" (Anne-Marie), "we have to go verify [the amount of workers exposed to dangerous radiations in the nuclear industry] as EDF is subcontracting on a large scale" (Anne-Marie), or in a question formulated by Eddy: "how should we fight against the lack of transparency in society when it comes to nuclear energy?", in which fighting for transparency is taken for granted as a desirable strategy.

The issue of social mobilization, demonstrations, and strikes on its own rights is discussed in the program aired on 12 December 2019, with Perrine, Sam and Patricia as participants. Like during the debate around *Vent de Bure*, the program also functioned as a space for debate and assessed the desirable and undesirable ways to organize, which they themselves and their student peers could make use of at future assembly or basic group meetings. Exclaiming "it scares me a lot", Patricia, a student participant, expresses her fears that, at a university, she can see "so many posters advertising events" like parties, "that seem rather useless compared to what happens at demonstrations and in the world". The depoliticization of university campuses and the focalization of student life on festive events, specifically at the UPEM (Université Paris-Est Marne-la-Vallée), revealed by the "students who, instead of being concerned with their situation are always partying" is "unfortunately a weakness", according to Sam. Patricia qualifies the university direction's strategy of organizing festive events with the help of student organizations, of a "shitty strategy". Sam carries on arguing that "this strategy" results in the following negative phenomena: "a very small amount students come to organize free coffee distributions", "apart from the politicized ones who know a bit the functioning of the unions", while the "worst is that some students are unaware of the fusion of the University and its consequences"; the "students elected in the administrative board" are negatively evaluated as opponents since they "are very close to the direction" "which is 200% pro-Macron" and "voted in favor of the fusion or abstained from the vote". Patricia negatively appraises ("it scares me") that "students aren't informed enough" and that "thirty people out of twelve thousand are organizing". She evaluates unions as "totally useful", as they intend to "rally" students go to demonstrate. Student unions' ways of organizing are also positively framed by Sam as they are "very creative when it comes to creating banners" and to "put stickers saying 'refugees welcome' ".

In this section, my analysis of the Radio LAP programs exposed that discourses about migration that are hegemonic in the political sphere and the media were dialogized by the participants in Radio LAP who ended up criticizing the nationalist and securitarian ideologies these discourses are caught in. The economic ideology was less subject to critique as migration was assumed to be a 'profitable' thing. The securitarian and antidemocratic approach of the nuclear energy question from the part of the French state institutions and French corporations was also polemicized by the Radio LAP participants, who unveiled its neo-colonial dimension as well when discussing the broader production context of nuclear raw materials like uranium. The identities that emerged during the events emphasized their rejection of police repression, of policies focused on generating and monopolizing profit in private hands, and affirmed the necessity of organizing in order to, for example, increase the importance of what can be characterized as welfare state prerogatives, such as the public good (energy in this case) and the protection of people (migrants in the context of this specific program).

References

Barot, Emmanuel. 2010. *Révolution dans l'Université: quelques leçons théoriques et lignes tactiques tirées de l'échec du printemps 2009*. Montreuil: Ville brûle.
Brown, Wendy. 2015. *Undoing the demos: Neoliberalism's stealth revolution*. Cambridge: MIT Press.
Chrisafis, Angelique. 2018. "We can't back down": French students dig in for macron battle. *The Guardian*, 5 April 2018, sec. World news. https://www.theguardian.com/world/2018/apr/05/we-cant-back-down-french-students-dig-in-for-macron-battle.
'Cinq choses à savoir sur "ExisTransInter", la marche des personnes trans et intersexes ce week-end'. 2019. *TÊTU* (blog). 18 October 2019. https://tetu.com/2019/10/18/cinq-choses-a-savoir-sur-existransinter-la-marche-des-personnes-trans-et-intersexes-ce-week-end/.
Delphy, Christine. 2015. *Separate and dominate: Feminism and racism after the War on Terror*. London: Verso.
Fairclough, Norman. 2003. *Analysing discourse: Textual analysis for social research*. London: Routledge.
Francke, Robin-Lee. 2019. Thousands protest in South Africa over rising violence against women. *The Guardian*, 5 September 2019, sec. World news. https://www.theguardian.com/world/2019/sep/05/thousands-protest-in-south-africa-over-rising-violence-against-women.
Graham-Harrison, Emma. 2017. Migrants from West Africa being "sold in Libyan slave markets". *The Guardian*, 10 April 2017, sec. World news. https://www.theguardian.com/world/2017/apr/10/libya-public-slave-auctions-un-migration.
La Croix. 2017. Emmanuel Macron veut faire de la France la « nation des start-up », 16 June 2017. https://www.la-croix.com/Economie/France/Emmanuel-Macron-veut-faire-France-nation-start-2017-06-16-1200855634.
'La Manif pour tous'. 2020. In *Wikipédia*. https://fr.wikipedia.org/w/index.php?title=La_Manif_pour_tous&oldid=168239174.

Laval, Christian, Francis Vergne, Pierre Clément, and Guy Dreux. 2011. *La nouvelle école capitaliste*. Paris: La Découverte.
'Marche des fiertés à Saint-Denis: "La banlieue aussi a une vie queer"'. 2019. *TÊTU* (blog). 31 May 2019. https://tetu.com/2019/05/31/marche-des-fiertes-a-saint-denis-la-banlieue-aussi-a-une-vie-queer/.
'Meuse/Haute Marne Underground Research Laboratory'. 2019. In *Wikipedia*. https://en.wikipedia.org/w/index.php?title=Meuse/Haute_Marne_Underground_Research_Laboratory&oldid=895639096.
Noiriel, Gérard. 2014. *Immigration, antisémitisme et racisme en France: (XIXe-XXe siècle) Discours publics, humiliations privées*. Paris: Fayard/Pluriel.
Rimbert, Pierre, and Serge Halimi. 2018. Not the world order we wanted. *Le Monde Diplomatique*, 1 September 2018. https://mondediplo.com/2018/09/01world-order.
Silverstein, Paul. 2018. *Postcolonial France: The question of race and the future of the republic*. London: Pluto Press.
Willsher, Kim. 2019. Unrest at French Universities after student sets himself alight over debts. *The Guardian*, 13 November 2019, sec. World news. https://www.theguardian.com/world/2019/nov/13/unrest-at-french-universities-after-student-sets-himself-alight-over-debts.

CHAPTER 5

Conclusion: Rethinking the Collective and the Individual in Education Through Self-Management: A Generalizable Endeavor?

Abstract Through an analysis of the interdiscursive aspects of the pedagogical practices of the school, I have found that the discourse of LAP tends to polemicize the French state's neoliberal discourse on education. In the pedagogical practices of LAP I analyzed, the tension between the teachers' and the students' agency was revealed. The issue of 'trust' between students and teachers in the construction of self-management practices was salient, as some teachers resorted to top-down practices foreclosing the emergence of practices in which students' agencies could fully develop. Yet, in the Radio LAP events, students were fully able to negotiate and realize the re-centering identity they wanted. Radio LAP participants were able to become the very 'gatekeepers' of the re-centering identity they deemed to be relevant, and 'authentic', according to the political struggles they choose to belong to and the collective social base these foreground.

Keywords Self-management • Critical pedagogy • Critical discourse studies • Dialogicity • Identity

The analysis demonstrated that the French State's official recontextualizing field, embodied by the Paris Academy at the regional level concerning LAP, is deeply caught in the managerial and market logics. In order to reach its instrumental goals of facilitating the student's insertion in the job market and of reinforcing the competitive advantage of the regional educational institutions, the academic project text promotes a managerial approach to the secondary education and clearly defines the various thinkable roles of the different actors of the educational institution and the hierarchy between them. The State's appropriate way of acting in relation to the educational system is argued to be one of a 'project builder', that is, a manager whose aim is to encourage 'innovation'. Evaluation takes place on the basis of 'good practices', naturalizing the 'thinkable' as 'good', which are practices valorizing 'success' in creating economic value mainly through cost-cutting.

The particular secondary institutions and their staff are supposed to adapt to the State-defined 'good practices' of economic success through finding ways to deal with the 'guidelines' ensuing from cost-reduction measures while providing equity for students in their 'professional insertion' as an objective through the development of 'project-based' pedagogical activities and the obtaining of particular skills, such as 'transversal' skills. As a replacement to public funding, 'partnerships' with other actors are argued to be relevant. However, combined with the adaptation to these economic changes concealed under the terms 'modernization' or 'progress', educational institutions are required to teach particular values identified with a fetishized idea of 'republic' through historical glorification and the silencing of 'inappropriate' religious behaviors. The combined appeal to market instrumentality and French nationalist narratives brings about two different types of appropriate pedagogical identities: a de-centered market identity focalized on exchange value at the market, and a centering (focused on past), 'fundamentalist' identity based on particular religious-nationalist myths, in this case, the 'secular French republic'. The 'republican' nationalist ideology intends to convey, successfully or not, a sense of belonging to an egalitarian entity that the market cannot provide. The ideology of secularism is racist as it specifically targets French citizens whose religion is Islam and represents them as not displaying enough 'love' toward the 'republic', thus blaming on their supposed rejection of 'republican values' the fact that they are not wholly considered part of the 'republic'.

5 CONCLUSION: RETHINKING THE COLLECTIVE AND THE INDIVIDUAL... 89

The different actors of the Paris Self-managed High School recontextualize the official discourse on education and its particular representations, genres and identities to shape their own representations, genres and identities by virtue of particular degrees of dialogicity. These degrees are combined in the specific pedagogical events taking place in LAP and vary according to the possible power relations shaping the agency of the participants and their context. According to Fairclough, the different degrees of dialogicity (discussed in Chap. 2) that can be combined in any event are the following:

> (a) an openness to, an acceptance of, recognition of difference; an exploration of difference, as in 'dialogue' in the richest sense of the term; (b) an accentuation of difference, conflict, polemic, a struggle over meanings, norms, power; (c) an attempt to resolve or overcome difference; (d) a bracketing of difference, a focus on commonality, solidarity; (e) consensus, a normalization and acceptance of differences of power which brackets or suppresses differences of meaning and norms. (Fairclough 2003, pp. 42–43)

Fairclough's scenario (e) entails the use of assumptions, where the ways of representing, acting and being from the perspective of a particular discourse are taken for granted and without explicit mention and are so recontextualized as 'natural' in another discourse. The instance of dialogicity combining taken for granted elements through assumptions is imposed by the superior authority of the neoliberal state leading to a consensus is salient in the process of applying to the school. Writing a CV and a motivation letter and going through a selection process of interviewing are instances of colonization by managerial practices at the level of the educational system. Other instances of colonization of pedagogical categories within a managerial discourse in LAP is the use of the word 'project' in the "Pedagogical project" document, for instance. The concept of 'project' is taken from the managerial discourse of new capitalism, to refer to (1) the school's pedagogical statement of value (the 'pedagogical project') and (2) to name particular pedagogical activities taking place in the school as 'projects'. In the former case, the reason is that it is a requirement for every school to comply with the rule of writing such a document in such form. Concerning the latter tendency of using 'project', the specific activities are articulated in terms of goals to be achieved by their completion. Although the goals are defined by the students themselves, the perspective of being evaluated and obtaining 'value units' or 'UV' (*unités de valeur*) as a reward for their achievement still articulates an instrumental dimension.

Scenario (e) is also noticeable with regard to the meaning of high school attendance, centered on the instrumental goal of obtaining the *baccalauréat*, albeit combined with scenario (b) as an opening of the possible purposes of attending high school. The discourse of LAP takes for granted that the dominant approach toward going to high school is to obtain the *baccalauréat* to be better 'integrated' in society. Because LAP is a state school, preparing students to pass the *baccalauréat* is its main requirement, and questioning this principle represents a threat to the very existence of the school. Yet, if the official discourse on education reduces 'success' in education to an instrumental approach consisting of obtaining value on the labor market through obtaining certificates like the *baccalauréat*, the discourse of LAP opens up the possible meanings of 'success' in education. In the discourse of LAP, success can be based on several criteria, and obtaining a degree is only one of them. For instance, success in education does not only involve the development of the individual's social value, generally reduced to its economic dimension by neoliberal discourse but also consists of the development of the political participation of the individual in collective political life. In turn, the critical pedagogic processes that will permit the conditions for this particular type of 'success' have to focus on teaching students to critically take part in collective choices through recognizing the different interests at stake. In the discourse of LAP, the meaning of educational success is thus broadened from depending on 'learning to become more valuable on the job market' toward 'learning to become a fully-fledged citizen'. The representation of pedagogical practices in LAP can re-appropriate the instrumental logic of the *baccalauréat*, for example, when a student argued that the technique of argumentation learnt during social movements can be useful in the perspective of passing the exam.

The dialogic scenario (b) in Fairclough's categorization was, however, predominant over the scenario (e) when the issue of the new *baccalauréat* law was discussed in the school. Unlike the configuration of the old *baccalauréat*, a fait accompli beyond discussion in LAP, the new *baccalauréat* configuration proposed by the Ministry of Education (Ministère de l'Education Nationale 2018) was not yet put into practice in the school at the time of my study. The reform, represented in the official recontextualization field as a natural 'evolution' to 'improve' the educational system, is recontextualized in the school discourse as a 'threat' since it is seen to impose evaluative mechanisms that put the existing pedagogical practices of LAP in danger. Teachers would become 'examiners' rather than 'pedagogues' and preparing students for the *baccalauréat* would entail a limitation of pedagogic freedom in favor of an increase in standardized testing and even an implementation of competitive devices such as student rankings. The recontextualization of the reform as a 'threat' to the school and its actors lead to its unanimous and categorical refusal inside LAP. Attempts to dialogue to resolve difference (scenario (c)) were intended with the Paris Academy, exposing the contradictions between a state discourse that foregrounds the 'free choice' and free agency of students in choosing their educational career and its authoritarian approach that focuses on cutting costs rather than taking into account the needs of the schools. Such attempts to resolve difference led to a delay in the implementation of the new law in the particular case of LAP, thereby postponing the conflict instead of resolving it.

The local pedagogic discourse of LAP represents the official discourse as limiting the 'thinkable' modalities of classification and framing in an authoritarian fashion. In LAP discourse, the official thinkable framing modalities are represented as obligations. In contrast, the weak framing modalities of the local pedagogic practices are expressed through an emphasis on a broader scope of available freedoms for students such as the 'freedom of attendance', and through the use of low deontic modality when representing the obligations incumbent upon participants of LAP. Also, 'traditional' ways of imposing discipline in schools are polemicized. They are assimilated to practices that are typical of criminal law enforcement, such as the likening of the 'internal regulations' (*règlement intérieur*) standard in 'traditional' schools, to a penal code. As an alternative to such disciplinary approaches likening students to potential 'criminals', the school includes self-management as a 'thinkable' pedagogical practice that does not entail obligations imposed by an arbitrary authority but by the necessities of the participation in a politically oriented community.

In the pedagogical practices of LAP I analyzed, tension between the teachers' and the students' agency could be observed. The issue of 'trust' between students and teachers in the construction of self-management practices was salient, as some teachers resorted to top-down practices foreclosing the emergence of practices in which students' agencies could fully develop. For instance, the student's attitude in what were represented by the teachers as the relevant social struggles was designated by the teachers as inappropriate 'passivity'. The relative absence of the student's voice in the discussions concerning the new *baccalauréat* reform translated a lack of interest against which teachers resorted to forms of authoritarian, top-down practices. In that particular case, teachers tried to impose a collective identity upon the students by emphasizing the fact that the school is a collective, and by resorting to further ways of building such an identity, for example, through calling up more events discussing and organizing the subsequent demonstrations at the grassroots level of the 'Basic Groups'.

It is telling that 'Basic Groups', which are the core of the 'bottom-up' processes of self-management in LAP, came to be instrumentalized by a specific purpose imposed by the teachers in the general assembly, in the name of resolving the matter of the so-called 'student passivity'. The divide is all the more visible as when students actively came up with the idea of creating a basic group for drug prevention, the relevance of which was already discussed beforehand among students, and they had to convince the teachers of the importance of such a group in a general assembly in order to have it built. When students relayed the calls of environmentalist collectives and collectives against police violence, they foregrounded a re-centering identity for which the collective social base was different from the social base of the 'union' calls foregrounded by teachers in a general assembly. In this particular case, the lack of discussion of these calls by the teachers in the general assembly leads to the foreclosing of the discussion at all. The identities negotiated in the general assemblies were re-centering identities as they backgrounded the instrumental purpose of improving the 'efficiency' of education to transmit a quantifiable and reified knowledge to individuals while foregrounding a collective social base. Yet, in the assemblies analyzed in my data, the teachers rather than the students were vested with a particular "gatekeepers and licensers' " authority to allow or deny the recognition of the 'authentic' re-centering identity by foregrounding the particular relevant political struggles and solidarities the group should be involved in (Bernstein 2000, p. 76), in this case, the struggle against the reform against the *baccalauréat*, threatening the immediate material interests of the school and of the teachers. The stigmatization of students mainly takes the form of labeling them as passive, and in the particular case of the justice commission, as 'subversive', implying that there *is* in fact an authority to subvert.

The stigmatizing labeling of students as 'passive' when they do not fit in the 'authentic' re-centering identity brought forward, sometimes by teachers in a top-down manner, was internalized by Céline. She argued in an interview that it took her time to realize that her so-called 'passivity' was what was preventing her from adapting to LAP and from thriving in her daily life at school. It is worth noting that her trajectory from a de-centered market identity embedded in the generic pedagogical model, toward the negotiation of a re-centering because of having to be integrated in the LAP collective, is still caught in an instrumental logic in which radical practices such as participating in demonstrations have the purpose of acquiring 'skills' relevant to pass the *baccalauréat* exam. In contrast, Antoine completely rejected the 'traditional' generic pedagogical model he had to suffer through and negotiated a form of re-centering identity against de-centered market identities in which value in the labor market is the dominant aspect. Instead, he argues enrolling in LAP allowed him to belong to a collective in which 'power with' practices made him feel empowered to act upon the world.

In the Radio LAP events, students were fully able to negotiate and realize the re-centering identity they wanted. Radio LAP participants were able to become the very 'gatekeepers' of the re-centering identity they deemed to be relevant, 'authentic', according to the political struggles they choose to belong to and the collective social base these struggles foreground. Practices of trust are more salient in the events as the teacher never imposed her own agency upon the orientation of the program. The principal limit of the Radio LAP project is that it is only representative of a minority of LAP's students. The students who chose to enroll in the Radio LAP project were mostly already adapted and thriving in the radical pedagogical model of LAP, and considered that they had something to *voice* in the radio program. Nevertheless, Radio LAP is the most relevant illustration in my data of the development of 'power with' pedagogical practices and of re-centering identities in a bottom-up approach.

The processes of re-centering identities negotiated by students in the Radio LAP program are the effect of the construction of a collective through their aim to build solidarities with particular political struggles beyond their immediate school context, which should foster conflicts with social groups whose representations were deemed illegitimate for various reasons. The representations of dominant social actors such as the government, corporations, right-wing political groups and mainstream media are rejected for justifying multiple forms of gender, race and class-based oppression. Instead, participants constructed approaches of solidarity with social groups identified as building forms of counter-hegemonic practices such as student unions or LGBTQI+ activist groups. The ultimate criterion at the core of the building of conflicts and solidarities is a material one: the different forms of oppression neoliberal capitalism and private profit entail are rejected across the pedagogical events, while demands for wealth redistribution in the perspective of empowering oppressed social groups and of resolving social issues, in general, are pushed forward. Students in the program not only negotiated re-centering identities through purely discursive means but embedded their counter-hegemonic discursive strategies in *praxis*, a dialectical combination of reflection and action. Indeed, for most programs, students situated themselves not only toward the social groups they expressed solidarity with, but also within, through participating in the actual events these groups organized *outside* the immediate field of pedagogical practice.

The purpose of my case study was to address the problem of the production, reproduction and critique of the neoliberal discourse of pedagogy in the Paris Self-managed High School (LAP), an educational institution self-identifying with critical pedagogy. I discussed how hegemony is articulated in the French educational system and how LAP situates itself with respect to hegemonic power relations. Through an analysis of the interdiscursive aspects of the pedagogical practices of the school, I have found that the discourse of LAP tends to polemicize the French state's neoliberal discourse on education. The managerial approach of banking pedagogy to education as 'efficient', that is, able to transmit reified individual 'skills' to individual students is generally framed as undesirable by LAP in favor of 'critical knowledge on a collective and democratic basis. Practices of solidarity with collectives situated in the broader context of the school are enacted through concrete action as well, such as participating in demonstrations or creating links of solidarity with various organizations. I have also shown that a limit to the democratic practices in the school emerges whenever the teachers' agency prevails over the students' in deciding which solidarities are desirable, such as during the struggle against the new *baccalauréat* reform, that is, when LAP needs to adopt to the new systems of evaluation of student's performance.

The legitimation of particular solidarities is articulated in the legitimation of particular identities. The analysis showed that the legitimate identities of neoliberal education, the competitive individualist subject, or the entrepreneurial student, are not generally encouraged in LAP's practices, as neoliberal hegemonic discourse is polemicized. Nonetheless, such identities can sometimes still be taken for granted in LAP due to the instrumental and individualizing requirement of the *baccalauréat* underlying most of the pedagogical practices. Instead, more 'radical' identities often came to be legitimized, foregrounding a potentially counter-hegemonic collective base with regard to acting on the world. Re-centering identities were negotiated by students in specific practices such as the Radio LAP program.

In contrast, in daily school practices, particular identities were occasionally encouraged by teachers on behalf of the students. My case study could show that the tension between the bottom-up and the top-down approaches to the creation of a collective and politicized base in the school's practices is the result of the micro-level power relations involved in the negotiation of the foregrounding and backgrounding of particular macro-level political issues in the pedagogical practices of LAP. However, individualistic but less competitive identities were also legitimized in some other pedagogical practices, for instance, when backgrounding the collective and political dimension of democratic education while foregrounding the self as a personal project facilitated by cooperative practices in which hierarchical relations are concealed.

The relative depoliticization of some students and teachers of LAP exposes the limits of the discussion of this case study. The radical aspect of the pedagogical practices discussed may be of concern only for the part of the school community that was the most visible during my time in LAP. In my fieldwork, after all, I focused on the teachers and students whose voices were the most present during the general assemblies, on students who volunteered to organize the Radio LAP program, and generally on any agent of the school community who thought had something relevant to say and did say it. My analysis concentrated on explaining the reasons behind the voices of some of the school's actors, and further research would be needed to understand the reasons behind the silence of others. Despite this limitation, my analysis has shown that the LAP school was an institution capable of fostering counter-hegemonic representations and identities by building collective practices of decision-making and by being involved in various kinds of struggles for social justice. In the present neoliberal context where competition is the common denominator of all social relations, for example competition for commodified skills, is the generalization of self-management in education a desirable step toward more social justice? The example of LAP suggests that this is the case.

REFERENCES

Bernstein, Basil. 2000. *Pedagogy, symbolic control, and identity.* Revised ed. Lanham: Rowman & Littlefield Publishers, Inc.

Fairclough, Norman. 2003. *Analysing discourse: Textual analysis for social research.* London: Routledge.

Ministère de l'Education Nationale. 2018. Baccalauréat 2021. https://cache.media.education.gouv.fr/file/BAC_2021/00/0/DP_BAC_BDEF_web_898000.pdf.

Index

A
Agency, 23, 25, 89, 91, 93, 94
Allegory, 53
Assumptions, 25
Austerity, 28, 50, 69

B
Baccalauréat, 26, 28, 48, 61, 70
Banking education, 26
Blanquer Law, 37, 39

C
Citizenship, 27
Comic strip, 50
Commodification, 18
Competition, 20
Critical pedagogy, 2, 3
Critical thinking, 2
Curriculum, 12, 24

D
Data sets, 7

Decision-making, 36
Decorative posters, 55
Deontic modality, 21, 45, 51, 55
Dialectics, 61–62
Dialogicity, 23–25, 32, 52, 71, 73, 75, 89
Dialogization, 51
Digital skills, 22
Discipline, 27, 44
Drug (prevention), 42

E
Energy (nuclear), 82
English (as a foreign language), 54
Evaluation, 15

F
Free choice, 68
Freedom of attendance, 46, 59

G
Gender, 71

Gendered violence, 75
Gender-neutral language, 73
General assembly, 36
Genre (of governance), 14
Good practices, 18
Grading, 42
Gramsci, Antonio, 4
Groupes de base, 36

H
Hate speech, 56
Hegemony, 23, 67
Hierarchical communication, 40
Horizontality, 30
Human capital, 13

I
Identification, 13
Ideology, 16
Individualizing discourse, 68
Interdiscursivity, 66
Intersectionality, 72, 74
Islam, 21

K
Knowledge economy, 14, 18, 22

L
LAP (functioning), 6
LGBTQI+ issues, 71–78
Literacy event, 5

M
Managerialism, 22, 23
Metaphor, 15
Migration, 79
Modality, 13
Modalization, 66

N
Neoliberalism, 12, 64
New Public Management, 17

P
'Power with,' 4, 24, 25, 40, 44, 60, 62, 93
Pride Banlieues, 72
Project, 15, 16, 20, 31, 47

R
Racism, 20
Recontextualization (of managerial practices), 38, 49
Recontextualizing field, 12
Refugee, 78
Republican values, 19, 20

S
Secularism, 21
Self-management, 47, 60

T
Technopreneurs, 22
Transphobia, 56
Transversal skills, 13, 29, 69, 88
Trust, 54

U
Une Fabrique de Libertés (book), 57

V
Value Units, 32
Vocational education, 16, 19

Y
Yellow Vests, 38

Printed in the United States
by Baker & Taylor Publisher Services